"Joseph R. Myers has written a multilayered, conversational book. [...] conversation, the content spurs you to discuss its theories with ot[...] ...ends, cowork- ers, neighbors, strangers—and as a result, you find yourself conversing with yourself about how true *The Search to Belong* is in your own life. Not only is it a fresh resource for ministry leaders grappling with the issues of biblical community in congregations, but it also proves helpful in navigating the complexities in our personal relationships."
—**Molly Cunningham, Congregational Community Development Practitioner, Cincinnati, Ohio**

"Many books are a rehash of known information. This book c[...] fresh ideas, and leads to untraveled roads. Reading *The Searc[...] mind and will stretch yours."
—**Rod Huron, Small Groups and Discipleship, Cincin[...]**

"This book needed to be written, and Joseph R. Myers has done an excellent job writing it. His examination of the four spaces in which "belonging" occurs will relieve and enlighten every Christian who has struggled with small groups. Even a quick overview will help increase the social capital of your spiritual community. Is *The Search to Belong* worth your time? It's the next book you must read!"
—**Chuck Smith jr., Senior Pastor, Capo Beach Calvary; Author,** *Epiphany: Discover the Delight of God's Word* **(Waterbrook Press)**

"Before your church jumps into the next fad diet of small group curriculum, you must read *The Search to Belong*. In a day where the Sunday "event" drives our churches and shrink-wrapped small group programs promise to deliver intimacy, Joseph R. Myers blows the doors off conventional thinking and offers a brilliant-yet-accessible approach to community."
—**Spencer Burke, Creator of TheOoze.com; Author,** *Making Sense of Church* **(emergentYS)**

"For all those who've been on guilt trips because they haven't a clue how to create inti- mate community—yet know community is part of the essence of Christianity—this book can provide deliverance. Combining sound sociological theory and solid biblical theology, Joseph R. Myers' *The Search to Belong* shows us how to evade the phoniness and fears that often accompany small group ministry and ministries in the life of the church. This is brilliant stuff."
—**Tony Campolo, Ph.D., Professor Emeritus of Sociology, Eastern University**

"Belonging is the topic de jour—and rightfully so. We need to feel an authentic connec- tion with others, or we will be physically, spiritually, and emotionally. Yet, over the last 50 years, the church seems to be losing more and more ground in the challenge to con- nect people in meaningful ways to church and even church-sponsored small groups. We keep applying the same remedies but don't seem to making any gains. *The Search to Belong* advances the ball on community. I read everything I can find on the subject, and Joseph R. Myers' interpretations greatly stimulated my thinking—and that will translate into concrete action in the days to come. Joseph R. Myers takes a meaty theory devel- oped in the 1960s ("proxemics") and translates it into worthy principles for our post- modern culture to consider. This isn't more of the same; it's something different—and thank goodness for that. In the opening chapter Myers writes, "This is a conversation, not a book of answers. So disagree. Argue. Wrestle with the thoughts presented." I, too, invite you to do just that."
—**Randy Frazee, Author,** *The Connecting Church* **(Zondervan); Senior Pastor, Pantego Bible Church, Ft. Worth, Texas**

"*The Search to Belong* takes an elegantly simple idea—that different kinds of space facili- tate different kinds of belonging—and explores its many rich applications to church life, ministry, and outreach. I've been "infected" with Joseph R. Myers' insight, and wish I had learned it 20 years ago! The book is a joy to read, and our churches will be better places if more of our leaders learn from him in these pages."
—**Brian D. McLaren, Pastor (crcc.org); Author,** *Adventures in Missing the Point* **(emergentYS);** *emergent fellow* **(emergentvillage.com)**

"For 20-plus years I've been encouraging church leaders to start small groups as the answer to community. It's been a sociological given that churchgoers want relationship. But almost all small group pastors I've known have pulled out their hair trying to get parishioners to attend groups. What's up with this inconsistency? Joseph R. Myers will guide you to a simple-yet-useful way to help people connect, understand their own confusion, and build community. By necessity you'll have to work your way though some introductory work, but read on—you'll be rewarded. The way people connect is changing at X-Games speeds, and leadership necessary to keep up will require the kinds of insights provided by *The Search to Belong*."
—Todd Hunter, Allelon Community of Churches; Former President, Vineyard-USA

"Joseph R. Myers will challenge your thinking about community in these pages. He not only raises the bar on the topic, he brings it to life like nothing I've ever read on the topic before. I highly recommend this book to everyone seeking to grow in the area of community."
—Steve Sjogren, Founding Pastor/Launching Pastor, Vineyard Community Church, Cincinnati, Ohio

"Skilled idea explorers not only travel to new places in their thinking, they also show us how to get there. In *The Search to Belong*, Joseph R. Myers provides a roadmap that helps us navigate the relational twists and turns among those in the church as well as connect authentically with those outside the church."
—Jim Henderson, Off the Map (www.off-the-map.org)

"*The Search to Belong* does many things. It relieves all of us who have never enjoyed the forced belonging of small groups from our guilt that we are "just not trying hard enough!" Joseph R. Myers also validates what so many have felt for years—that the small group movement is not all it was touted to be. Small groups were promoted as the end game when, in fact, they are a means to many things if allowed to blossom, based on the tenor of the groups as opposed to the icebreaker and lesson plans for that week. This book is not just for the church—it's for anyone in a relationship or seeking to understand the dynamics of belonging.

The metaphor of the front porch is (for me at least) the best part of the book. First, it took me on a stroll down memory lane to the hours and hours I spent on the front porch as a child. I was reminded of the security I felt, the tender moments shared, both with grandparents, friends, and those passing by, and how safe it felt not only to be on my front porch, but also on anyone else's. Second, it gave me an entirely new lens to look through as I view my own church, as well as all the others I come in contact with. I now look to see where the "front porch" is, for it's where initial safety and belonging are found.

Thank you for writing this gentle and thoughtful book. Rather than being prescriptive or even descriptive, *The Search to Belong* provides us with the tools for reflection, both personally and corporately, and allows us to find the right conclusions for our environments."
—Sue Mallory, Author, *The Equipping Church* (Zondervan)

"Finally, an understanding of community that hits us where we really live. *The Search to Belong* has opened my eyes and heart to a deeper and more thoughtful understanding of community. It tears down the stereotype that you have to be "plugged into a group" to experience belonging and community—because, as Joseph R. Myers writes, community is really all around us. You have to read this material!"
—Murphy Belding, Small Group Pastor, Southeast Christian Church, Louisville, Kentucky

"A simple insight (your true "belongings" are not your possessions, but the people to whom you belong and who belong to you) leads Joseph R. Myers to some of the most revolutionary and original thinking about small groups in the church today. Don't read this book if you're not open to fundamental more than fiddly changes in how to build the body of Christ."
— Leonard Sweet, Drew Theological School, George Fox University, preachingplus.com

the SEARCH to BELONG

RETHINKING INTIMACY,
COMMUNITY,
AND SMALL GROUPS

JOSEPH R. MYERS

Forewords by
coach **JOHN WOODEN**
& futurist **LEONARD SWEET**

ZONDERVAN.COM/
AUTHOR**TRACKER**

GRAND RAPIDS, MICHIGAN 49530

Youth Specialties products, 300 South Pierce Street, El Cajon, CA 92020, are published by Zondervan, 5300 Patterson Avenue, Southeast, Grand Rapids, MI 49530

Library of Congress Cataloging-in-Publication Data

Myers, Joseph R., 1962–
  The search to belong : rethinking intimacy, community, and small
groups / Joseph R. Myers.
      p. cm.
  ISBN-10: 0-310-25500-7 (pbk.)
  ISBN-13: 978-0-310-25500-0 (pbk.)
  1. Community—Religious aspects—Christianity. 2. Small
groups—Religious aspect—Christianity. 3. Intimacy
(Psychology)—Religious aspects—Christianity. I. Title.
  BV4517.5.M94 2003
  262'.2—dc21

                                                    2003005789

Web site addresses listed in this book were current at the time of publication. Please contact Youth Specialties via e-mail (YS@YouthSpecialties.com) to report URLs that are no longer operational and replacement URLs if available.

Some of the anecdotal illustrations in this book are true and are included with the permission of the persons involved. All other illustrations are composites of true situations, and any resemblance to people living or dead is coincidental.

Edited by Randy Frame
Cover and interior design by Electricurrent
Cover photo by Michael Wilson

Printed in the United States of America

09 • 10 9

+ *Dedication*

To Kennon L. Callahan, whose great wisdom has yielded many helpful discoveries. This book would not have been possible without his coaching. I can barely imagine how different my life would be without Ken's help and compassionate friendship. Dr. Callahan has made my life—and the life of my family—richer and fuller by giving us, among many other things, the gift of knowing there are many possibilities.

+ *Special Thanks*

I thank those communities where I belong.

I thank my family, which taught me well.

I thank my wife, Sara, who shares her wisdom and love as we grow together. She allows the flexibility and freedom to belong in all the spaces. (Sara, you make lovin' fun.) Sara has poured many hours into reworking this book. She is among the best editors in the world. But I thank her mostly for her wise questions and her willingness to listen.

Thanks to Jaclyn, my daughter, for teaching me how to be a father. I am proud to be your father.

I thank my mother, who loves me unconditionally. And my father, who has shown me the value of wisdom.

I thank my siblings, who teach me grace and mercy.

Thanks to my mother-in-law for her undying encouragement and helpful stories. And to my father-in-law, a good writing coach and friend.

I thank my uncle Don for being more like an older brother and for the fun of being friends.

I thank the family at settingPace for their hard work, encouraging words, and friendship.

I thank the community that gathers at Callaway every spring to grow, reflect, and have fun. And Ken Callahan for his unending wisdom and friendship.

Thanks to those at theooze.com. The journey is richer because of you. Spencer, you are a compassionate friend.

Thanks to Dave and Catherine, who are true neighbors wherever they live.

Thanks to those friends who have enriched *The Search to Belong* through their helpful encouragement and insightful questions—Jon, Jim, Jonathan, John, Heather, Dwight, Stephanie, Molly, Todd, Bill, and Doug.

Thanks to the Indiana University men's basketball program. I am glad and honored to be a fan.

Thanks to the publishing community. You have provided many opportunities for dreams to develop.

Thanks to emergentYS and to the *emergent village*. Your courage is an encouragement. MarkO, Brian, Len, and Doug, thanks for believing in this material. And thanks to Dave and Randy for making my words more readable.

Finally, thanks to the many congregations that let me drop in and join the family conversation.

+ *Author Note*

This book is filled with wisdom gathered from research, interviews, and anecdotal observation. Most of these insights are shared through story. Every story is true. And if a story sounds like it is your story, it probably is—yours and a thousand others. I have often chosen to merge several stories into one. This makes each story everyone's story, but no one's individual story.

I have included the discoveries that will help begin a new community conversation. But some discoveries did not fit, and others are yet to be made. Thus, I would enjoy hearing from you to further this discussion.

Joe Myers
jmyers@languageofbelonging.com
Or join the conversation on the message boards at
www.languageofbelonging.com

+ Contents

+ *Foreword*

Coach John Wooden

When people begin to discuss the teams I coached, they quickly attribute our success to individual talent.

Nothing could be further from the truth.

I tell them the same thing I told my players at UCLA: we, as a team, are like a powerful car. Maybe a Bill Walton or Kareem Abdul-Jabbar is the big engine, but if one wheel is flat, we're going nowhere. And if we have brand new tires but the lug nuts are missing, the wheels come off. What good is the powerful engine now? It's no good at all.

A lug nut may seem like a little thing, but it's not. Each part of the car plays an important role—and it's the same way in our lives. Success isn't about individual talent. Success comes from the power of *team*. And we cannot achieve anything together until we fulfill the roles we're assigned. Even if our roles are "little"—because it's the "little" things that make big things happen.

But what is the secret to *team*? How do we lose ourselves for the good of the group? Gifted players who aren't team players ultimately hurt the team, whether it revolves around basketball or business or the church.

And great teams are filled with players who understand that the good of the group comes first. But this understanding and sacrifice happens only when each player experiences belonging.

Joseph R. Myers has opened a new door to help us understand this in *The Search to Belong*.

When I coached, I spent a lot of time and energy trying to understand and implement the secrets of team chemistry. Joseph has shown me why some of the ideas I tried where successful and why some were not.

The one thing that I know contributed to my teams meshing together—and it's something Joseph emphasizes throughout this book—is that all players must be valued.

All members of your team must know they're wanted, needed, and appreciated. And it's the leader's job to help them experience value through their experience of belonging.

If you're in a position where helping people to experience belonging and community is your responsibility, this is a book full of insights and simple, real-life understanding. *The Search to Belong* helps us to answer: We are many...but are we much?

—John Wooden, former coach of the record-setting UCLA men's basketball team, won 10 national championships in 12 years.

+ *Foreword*

Leonard Sweet

But for two interventions, tonight I would be eking out an existence playing "Moon River," "Moonlight Sonata," and other requests on the piano while you and yours are eating Chilean Sea Bass (the dressy name for Patagonian tooth-fish) at some upscale restaurant.

First were the words of my high school band director, Mr. Norman Clo. "Pianists are a dime a dozen," he warned one day after rehearsal as he picked up his French horn. "Unless you're prepared to practice seven hours a day, don't even think about it."

But these words, spoken when I announced my intention of attending Juilliard School of Music, were not enough to keep me from my self-anointed future. In fact, given my stiffening state of adolescent defiance, these words were more like catnip beckoning me to a future on the bench.

The things that really kept me from the life of a professional pianist were Marilyn and her magic fingers. Marilyn and I were exact opposites in almost every way. I was Methodist, Marilyn was Baptist. I was 6'4" and 150 lbs; Marilyn was 5'4" and 250 pounds. Twice my age, Marilyn was also twice the pianist.

I could sight-read almost any piece of music. Marilyn only played by ear. In one of Gary Larson's *The Far Side* cartoons, a French horn player is sitting in the middle of a symphony orchestra during a concert. Pointing at the sheet music on his stand, he says, "Gee, look at all the little black dots!" Marilyn couldn't decipher a dot or read a note, but she could play any piece of music, picking out of the air a phrase, turning it inside out, then upside down, and making a shard into a symphony.

Because I could read dots, I was chosen to play "Rhapsody in Blue" with a full orchestra behind me. But every soloist or instrumentalist wanted Marilyn as accompanist. Only if they couldn't get Marilyn did they want me.

No matter how skilled at "sight reading" I became, I never could "play it by ear." And even in my teen state of darkness, I sensed that sight knowledge was shallow compared to sound knowledge. *If you can't turn an eye into an ear*, an inner voice told me, *don't go to Juilliard*.

The literature on small groups is vast—and maturing. But most of it is written by people possessing only varying degrees of sight-reading skill. Joseph R. Myers' *The Search to Belong* is the first book written by an artist who's truly "hearing it into vision." A simple insight—your true "belongings" are not your possessions, but your relationships—leads Myers to some of the most revolutionary and original thinking about small groups and spatial competencies in the church today.

Don't read this book if you're not open to more fundamental than fiddly changes in how the church builds community. Don't read this book if you're not prepared to help your church dance the night away.

—Leonard Sweet, Drew University, George Fox University, preachingplus.com

+ *Those Who Show Up Along the Way*
(an introduction)

Looking for someone? We all are. But who? We don't want to be alone. But when it comes to belonging, we're confused. And our culture is confused. We are together, all alone.

If there is one conversation with which the emerging church must wrestle in new ways, it is the question, "Who is my neighbor?" Who belongs? For whom am I responsible? And who is responsible to me? How can we help people develop a healthy experience of belonging and community in their lives?

These are the guiding questions of *The Search to Belong*. This book focuses largely on the language we use (both verbal and non-verbal) to communicate to others a sense of belonging or the lack thereof.

The Search to Belong is part self-help. Discovering new ways of understanding what it means to belong will help us value and enrich our relationships with our spouses and families as well as others with whom we interact.

The Search to Belong is also part church-help. One of the major goals of this book is to provide a language to begin a new conversation about how congregations can assist people in their fundamental search to belong.

We live in a culture that now prioritizes belonging over believing. Pastors and key leaders sense that they need to adjust their language in order to adapt to this cultural shift. The question is, "How?" *The Search to Belong* suggests a framework for change.

This book is a practical guide for those who struggle to build a community of believers. I invite you to question and challenge the ways in which the church and culture have defined and promoted "healthy community."

During my research, I discovered that architects, sociologists, city planners, human resource developers, psychologists, scientists, and pastors provided insights to help with the community puzzle. But most of all, those with whom I have bonded connected the pieces. Those from my past and those to whom I now belong are a part of a personal inventory I call my community.

In *The Search to Belong*, I don't search for the answer. Instead, I offer a framework—a language of belonging—to describe how we can discover healthy connections naturally. There is a continuum of possibilities for community, as opposed to a single prescription.

I am indebted to the work of Edward T. Hall. His groundbreaking studies provide a foundation for discussing community and belonging in the various "spaces" of our lives: public, social, personal, and intimate.

The Search to Belong shares stories that illustrate how to help people connect more authentically with family, with congregation, and with God. This new language of belonging—which represents new ways of conceptualizing our relationships—helps people describe their connections and supports individuals and congregations in their quest for health.

In fact, I believe that as words such as "family," "neighbor," and "friend" are redefined, we may need to find a new definition for those who encompass "congregation." And, invite all those who connect to join the conversation.

As you read, look for those who belong to you. You might be surprised at who shows up along the way.

[*one*]

the myths of belonging

Our old ideas about space have exploded. The past three decades
have produced more change in more cultures than any other time in
history. Radically accelerated growth, deregulation, and globalization
have redrawn our familiar maps and reset the parameters: Borders are
inscribed and permeated, control zones imposed and violated, jurisdictions declared
and ignored, markets pumped up and punctured. And at the
same time, entirely new spatial conditions, demanding new definitions,
have emerged. Where space was considered permanent, it now feels
transitory—on its way to becoming. The words and ideas of architecture,
once the official language of space, no longer seem capable of describing
this proliferation of new conditions. But even as its utility is questioned
in the real world, architectural language survives, its repertoire of concepts
and metaphors resurrected to create clarity and definition in new,
unfamiliar domains (think chat rooms, Web sites, and firewalls). Words that
die in the real are reborn in the virtual.[1]

Rem Koolhaas, in a guest editorial for a special issue of *Wired*

When our pastor rose to make the announcement, I suspected we were in for it again. "We're going to be a church *of* small groups," he told us, like a child pleading for his parents to read from the well-worn book one more time. "A church *of* small groups instead of a church *with* small groups."

My heart sank. Been there; done that.

I remembered attending a small group several years earlier. It was the next step in my process of growing deeper in Christ and in community. "Everyone in a small group" was the church-wide goal. So my wife, Sara, and I hopped in our car and began our eight-week commitment.

We were greeted kindly at the door. It was not so much a friendship sort of kind as it was a salesman's type. "This is the first time," I told myself, "so relax and enjoy."

9

Once gathered in the "family" room, we played several silly, juvenile games in the hope of opening the door to relational bliss. Next, we were asked to agree to and sign a Group Covenant.

The covenant seemed harmless enough. It established a purpose for the group. It enlisted everyone to the 100 percent attendance policy. It explained a code of group life. It requested that we enter into accountable relationships with our new "friends."

The covenant was very organizational and institutional. Its purpose, values, and vision were all clearly stated. Everyone signed on the line. Our well-trained leader promised that eight weeks later we would all arrive at a closer walk with God and with one another.

Sounded promising and hopeful, so we started. By the third week I had had enough. I did not want to return to share my deepest thoughts. I did not want to give obvious answers to predictable questions from the published small group material. I did not want to play one more icebreaker game.

I was not getting closer to anyone. Instead, I was getting angry. This group was expecting more from me than I wanted to deliver. And this group was trying to deliver to me more than I wanted.

A church of small groups? Sounded like forced relational hell to me.

Others tell of similar experiences. When a friend asked Miguel to help start a men's small group for the new year, he agreed at once. Through a contact in the hotel business, Miguel found the ideal meeting place and time: Holiday Inn at 6:30 a.m. on the second and fourth Tuesdays. The men would meet for breakfast, pray, read from a study book, and by 7:30 be on their separate ways to work.

The group was launched and continued through the spring, summer, fall, and even the winter. Sometimes as few as four gathered, sometimes as many as seven. Every second and fourth Tuesday at 6:30 a.m., often on cold and dark mornings, they met. Through vacations, travel schedules, traffic tie-ups, the group met.

As the second summer approached, someone suggested, "Let's take a breather for a few months." Everybody agreed. When September arrived, not one person suggested starting again.

+ *Common Myths of Belonging*

Community is a complex creature. Many factors contribute to finding successful community. With the erosion of the geographically close family and the heightened mobility of our culture, many people struggle to learn healthy competencies for community.

Schools, service agencies, churches, and other organizations are making a concerted effort to help. Yet several common myths surround the search to belong, myths that dilute and confuse the definitions we employ to describe our journey to connect.

More time = more belonging. The first myth is that the greater the amount of time spent in relationship with another person, the more authentic the community will be. This is a pervasive myth. In reality, time has little to do with a person's ability to experience significant belonging. Many people tell stories of first-time, episodic introductions from which a spontaneous connection emerges. Have you ever said, "I just met you, but it seems like I've known you all my life."

Contrast this with Teri's feelings about Maggie. The two roomed together in college years ago, and ever since have exchanged Christmas cards and the occasional letter. Last summer Maggie invited herself to spend a few days with Teri.

When Teri got the phone call, she immediately went to her pastor. "I didn't like her then," she groaned. "I put up with her. Her side of the room was always filthy. She's domineering. I don't want her to come here. What do I do? We roomed together for four years, but we were never really friends."

Or, for still another perspective, Rose describes an experience at her church:

> About a month ago a woman named Sandra began attending. She is 56 years old. She came to our group last night. She has zero church background. Four years ago she was alone on a week-long vacation to Mexico. One morning by the pool, she struck up a conversation with the young woman sitting next to her. She learned that this young woman was there on her honeymoon. When the bride's husband joined her by the pool, Sandra tried to excuse herself, but they just kept talking with her.

Sandra said that off and on during the rest of her vacation, she ran into this couple. They mentioned they attended a Vineyard church in California. Sandra was quick to mention to me, "It wasn't like they were trying to recruit me or anything; it just came up in one of our conversations that they were Christians and where they went to church."

Sandra was so impressed with how kind they were, and she liked how they treated each other. She went away from them thinking they had something—values or a lifestyle—she found attractive.

She told me probably once a year for the past four years she has thought about going to church. She looked in the phonebook for a Vineyard church (because she had no idea where else to go) and found us.[2]

A short connection around a swimming pool had significance years later. Belonging is not controlled by time, and time *by itself* does not develop belonging.

More commitment = more belonging. People often believe that there is a significant relationship between *commitment* and *community*. This is, however, a romantic view. When we search to belong, we aren't really looking for commitment. We simply want to connect.

A relationship that involves commitment does not necessarily promote a greater experience of belonging. A married couple may feel very committed to their relationship, yet still feel the strain of "not belonging to each other." Every month I am reminded of my commitment to my financial responsibilities, yet I never experience belonging because of those commitments.

I have similarly observed that people equate *close* relationships with *committed* relationships. They use words such as "authentic," "deep," or "intimate" to express significance. And since we are all searching for significant connection, we fool ourselves into a pattern of trying to make all or most relationships *close*, sometimes in inappropriate ways.

To experience healthy community we need significant relationships. "Significant" is not the same as "close" or "committed." My wife, Sara, practices the ancient craft of rug hooking. "Hookers," as they call themselves, gather around the country in small guilds, in weeklong schools, and for conferences. Every fall Sara attends a

weekend conference in northern Ohio. This conference is very significant in Sara's life. She finds help with her craft. She connects
with those who have the same passion. Mostly, she finds a respite
from her busy life. Yet neither the relationship with the conference
nor the relationship with the participants can be accurately called
"committed."

Sara is by no means committed to the conference. Every year
the discussion is repeated: "Should I spend the money and time or
should I stay home?" Even though she has attended several years in a
row, the conference cannot count on her commitment. What they
can count on is her passion for the craft. And that she will make her
decision to attend at the very last moment.

She has no committed relationship with any of the participants.
She is just now beginning to remember their names from year to
year. She rarely connects with them outside of the conference. She
has never called any of them on the phone to chat.

These relationships cannot be described as close or committed.
Still, they are significant to Sara's healthy experience of community.

> People come to a church longing for, yearning for, hoping for this
> sense of roots, place, belonging, sharing, and caring. People come to a
> church in our time with a search for community, not committee.
> We make the mistake of assuming that, by putting people on a
> committee, they will develop ownership for the objectives of the
> church. People are not looking for ownership of objectives or for
> functional, organizational, institutional goals. Their search is far more
> profound and desperate than that. They are looking for home, for
> relationships. They are looking for the profound depths of community.[3]
>
> **Kennon L. Callahan, *Effective Church
> Leadership: Building on the Twelve Keys***

More purpose = more belonging. During the 1980s Tom
Peters led *The Search for Excellence* revolution within the business
community. Mission, vision, and purpose statements were pre-
scribed to ailing and healthy organizations alike. Groups were started
to help people with their search for community, and the first order
of business was to write a statement of purpose. After all, people
who strive together toward a common goal connect, right?

We even changed our language. We no longer asked people to attend *committee* meetings. They were now part of a *team*. And this simple change was all in the hope of helping people connect in significant ways.

Although many positive accomplishments sprang from this newly focused approach, in reality this strategy has very little connection with the community experience. Sometimes people who have a common passion and purpose *do* connect. But a common

"Abandon Committees,
Skip Teams and
Embrace Communities"

Does it seem to you that congregations are late adapters to some trends? It does to me. It appears at times that congregations are just getting around to adapting to certain trends as the next trend is emerging. For example, organizing congregations according to teams rather than committees is now in its ascendancy, just as in the world at-large, teams are fading in favor of communities.

It is a positive step that congregations are abandoning committees for teams, but what if congregations were to skip the team phase and embrace communities? Too radical? Perhaps so! Too cutting edge? Hardly!

Leadership communities and learning communities are the next wave of congregational governance and empowerment. Are you ready? Consider these seven differences between committees, teams, and communities as you think about making the transition:

Difference One—**Formation:** Committees tend to be elected or appointed in keeping with the bylaws, policies, or polity of congregations. Teams are recruited or drafted to work on a specific task or set of tasks. Communities are voluntarily connected in search of genuine and meaningful experiences.

Difference Two—**Focus:** Committees focus on making decisions or setting policies. Teams focus on maturing to the point that they become high task performance groups.

Communities add qualitative relationships, meaning, and experiences to the organizations, organisms, or movements to which they are connected.

Difference Three—**Membership:** Committees tend to have a fixed term of membership. Teams may have a defined term of membership, or may serve until a certain set of tasks is completed. Communities have no bounded membership and people tend to come and go based on their continuing interest in the journey.

Difference Four—**Outside Assistance:** Committees seek high quality training events or consultants, if they need outside assistance. Teams partner with respected practitioners or coaches. Communities align with champions or advocates who come alongside them in long-term relationships.

Difference Five—**Recruitment:** Committees look for people of position who can bring to the committee or council influence to get the work of the committee respected by people of power in the congregation. Teams look for people of expertise who have the gifts, skills and preferences to complete a certain task or set of tasks. Communities look for people of passion who want to have fun helping to bring exciting experiences to congregational participants, and a spiritual strategic journey to the congregation.

Difference Six—**Benefits:** Committees benefit congregations by building ownership and loyalty for the mission of the congregation. Teams benefit congregations by providing more effective action more quickly than committees. Communities benefit congregations by providing more enthusiasm and meaningful relationships within congregations.

Difference Seven—**Style of Work:** Committees focus on making decisions that are lasting and manage the resources of the congregation efficiently at the best price. Teams focus on debating the strengths and weaknesses of the various choices to complete a task, and typically end up with the highest quality product or outcome. Communities dialogue, engage in discernment activities, and arrive at the best solutions for a particular opportunity or challenge.

Is your congregation ready to embrace communities?[4]

George Bullard, "Abandon Committees, Skip Teams and Embrace Communities"

purpose or vision or goal does not guarantee that people will connect.

More personality = more belonging. Many people believe that some have a natural ability to belong. They assume that if a person is more gregarious, more extroverted, he or she will have little trouble experiencing community, whereas those who are shy will struggle to belong.

This misconception is based on an outward perception of what is taking place. It has very little to do with what is actually experienced. I have interviewed several extroverts who outwardly seem to have little trouble connecting, yet who speak of a deep search for belonging. I have listened also to those who are shy tell me that their lives are rich and full with significant community.

For example, Dave has for several years been the leading salesperson in his company. No sooner do you meet Dave than it becomes obvious why he is so successful at his job. Dave has never met a stranger. He is outgoing. He is neither fake nor obnoxious. He is genuine and interesting, able to bring people into a conversation with great ease and make them feel welcome. Yet when I talk with Dave about life, he says he wishes things were different.

"Different?" I inquired.

"I wish I could develop friendships," Dave replied.

"Friends? You have many friends!" I reminded him.

"No, not really," he told me. "I have people who are comfortable around me. I am not comfortable around them. That's why I am so outgoing. I'm scared they will not like me. I'm scared they do not like me."

Michelle thinks Dave is a really great guy. Michelle is an introvert; she describes herself as quiet and a bit shy. "I'm not painfully shy," she explains. "I just don't speak up. I like to listen. I get a lot of energy from listening. I also like to be by myself. I enjoy time alone. People seem to drain me."

"Do you find it difficult to make friends?" I asked.

"No. I have a lot of friends." She continued, "I have a few friends from high school that I still get together with."

"Do you wish you could work a room like Dave?" I asked.

"No," she replied. "I am content with the way I am. I like Dave, but that would wear me out."

Introversion and extroversion are learned forms of social behavior that help us navigate our day-to-day lives. They are categories for helping us understand and interpret our relational experiences. But introversion and extroversion neither block nor enhance our experience of belonging. Healthy community can be experienced and developed by introvert and extrovert alike.

More proximity = more belonging. Remembering a time when the culture was less mobile than it is today, people tend to believe the fifth myth: geographical proximity creates greater community. Says Randy Frazee, "The simple fact is that in all places of effective community people live in close proximity to each other."[5]

> We think of belonging as permanence, yet all our homes are transient. Who still lives in the house of their childhood? Who still lives in the neighbourhood [sic] where they grew up? ...
> Our belonging is no longer to something fixed, known and familiar, but to an electric and heartless creature eternally in motion.[6]
>
> **Michael Ignatieff, *The Needs of Strangers***

This statement is both true and false. It is true that people who live in close geographical proximity may connect with one another. Yet space is in some sense a matter of perspective. The same real estate can convey a certain distance in one situation yet have an entirely different meaning in another. *(We will expand on this in chapter 3, Give Me Some Space).*

Further, "close proximity" need not be geographical. Consider, for example, the significant connections that are made digitally. Online bulletin boards and chat rooms, instant messaging, and mobile phone text messaging do not require close proximity to establish significant connections among people.

More small groups = more belonging. I have often heard ministers say to their congregations, "We're glad you're here. But if you really want to know what it's like to be part of our congregation, participate in a small group."

The implication is that small groups are the best—if not the only—way to build authentic community. Almost every book I read on developing a successful church touts small groups as the key. But I have read that churches that provide small group opportunities can expect about a 30 percent involvement at best from the congregation

Why only 30 percent? Because small groups do not accomplish the promise of fulfilling all facets of a person's search for community. Small groups deliver only on one or two specific kinds of connection. A person's search for community is more complex than this. The truth is that people can experience belonging in groups ranging in size from two to 2,000 or more. People have the competencies to pursue many different paths in their search for community. Many congregations have gone down the small group road only to find they have circled a cul-de-sac and ended up where they began.

[
Today, the idea of space employs more movement and goes beyond the visual to a much deeper sensual space.[7]

Edward T. Hall, *The Hidden Dimension*]

This is not a book about small groups, though in the current church culture, one cannot adequately discuss community without addressing the small group craze. For the record, I am not against small groups. I am actually very much in favor of them. But I am against small groups being used and marketed as the "end-all" solution for answering the individual's search to belong. Perhaps this was best expressed by the participant in a small group's roundtable who observed, "It is too small to think just small group."

Probably, most of us have bought into one or more of these six myths, whether wittingly or unwittingly. And most of us have probably been left feeling like we've been cheated out of a promise. I know I have. And so I began to search for an authentic description of "belonging" in order to enhance the "community conversation." And I began to search for the place belonging plays in the conversation of my life.

+ *An Epiphany*

Attending a conference, I sat in a room listening to Len Sweet and Brian McLaren discuss how postmodern persons wish to "belong before they believe." Most participants shook their heads in affirmation. This bothered me. It was not the validity of the statement, but rather the fashion in which we all agreed with it that disturbed me. Did we really know what we were agreeing to?

I'd read and heard this phrase before. I believe the statement accurately represents a major shift in how we are going to communicate to the emerging culture. I had already come to the conclusion that the time we could by argument convince someone they should "come on board" was gone. But it seemed we were forming a consensus too easily, even smugly, on the definition of "belonging."

[
The future of the church depends on whether it develops true community. We can get by for a while on size, skilled communication, and programs to meet every need, but unless we sense that we belong to each other, with masks off, the vibrant church of today will become the powerless church of tomorrow. Stale, irrelevant, a place of pretense where sufferers suffer alone, where pressure generates conformity rather than the Spirit creating life—that's where the church is headed unless it focuses on community.[8]

Larry Crabb in the foreword of *The Connecting Church*
]

Most of us have always believed that a person could "belong" as long as their definition of belonging agreed with ours. Most of us have been raised on a healthy dose of believing before belonging. For others to belong, to "join the club," it was a prerequisite that the person subscribe to our belief system.

But this definition did not seem to match Sweet and McLaren's. More importantly, it did not match the emerging culture's definition. This haunted me in my sleep. What does it mean to "belong before we believe?" How *do* we communicate "belonging"? And how *should* we? In holding to the truths of our faith, can we allow people to belong before they know or fully understand what they are getting themselves into? Or better yet, what would we be getting into ourselves if we allowed just *anyone* to belong?

Because I was teaching a class in public speaking at a nearby college, I missed the final session of Sweet and McLaren's conference. The agenda for my class that morning was to discuss communication theories surrounding the work of Edward T. Hall.

Hall, in the 1960s, developed a theory based on the relationship between space and culture, specifically how spaces affect the culture of living matter. Hall coined the term *proxemics* "for the interrelated observations and theories of man's use of space."[9] He concluded that there are four spaces we use to develop personalities, culture, and communication. Those spaces are: public, social, personal, and intimate:[10]

Space Reference Distance

Public	12 feet +
Social	4 to 12 feet
Personal	18 inches to 4 feet
Intimate	0 to 18 inches

As I wrote on the board and gave a brief description of each, I said, "These four spaces communicate how we belong to each other." There it was. I am sure I had said it many times before when presenting Hall's discoveries. But this time my statement birthed an entirely new meaning, perhaps for students, but definitely for me. If what I said was true, could this concept of spaces be a clue, perhaps a vehicle for exploring the questions Sweet and McLaren had stirred?

I stopped in mid-sentence, staring at what I had written on the board. The pause got my students' attention. I wondered aloud: "Could this mean that belonging is multidimensional? Might people belong to us on different levels?"

One of my students, not realizing that I was really asking the question to myself, answered, "Of course." There followed a rich, full discussion. I listened to a roomful of postmodern students discuss the "simple complexities" of what it means to belong.

Specifically, we discussed what it means to belong to institutional organizations and social structures, formal and informal. We discovered that Hall had given us a tool to discuss the dimensions of belonging. He had supplied a framework for communicating in a new way: the language of belonging.

Inductively we discovered that Hall's work not only supplied a structure for architecture and city planning (space = real estate), culture, and communication, but his concepts of space also applied to the conversation about belonging. This is a conversation about recognizing, describing, and validating (or invalidating) the ways in which we build healthy community and employ specific spaces to communicate belonging.

[
The development of meaningful relationships where every member carries a significant sense of belonging is central to what it means to be the church.[11]

Randy Frazee, _The Connecting Church_
]

My hope is that you will become more aware of the language we use and how it can communicate belonging and build community. I hope further that we can all expand our definitions of belonging and community to include those whom God has given us in mission. May the process find us effectively conversing with the people Jesus misses most.

Work through this book, then, with a healthy sense of progress and peace, knowing that God is with us and, more importantly, with "them."

+ [*consider*]

+ Which of the myths have you discovered in your search to belong? Have you discovered any others? Have you conveyed these myths as truths?

+ How has the cultural shift to "belonging before believing" affected your life and congregation?

+ Write a definition/description of what it means to belong in each of the four spaces.

[*two*]

longing to belong

[Americans] are among the loneliest people in the world.[1]
George Gallup Jr., *The People's Religion*

I n the second grade I was Jon's best friend, although it was news to me. I'm not sure how this happened. Mrs. King, our second-grade teacher, gave us an assignment to write a report and read it to the class. The report was to be titled "Can You Guess Who My Best Friend Is?" Mrs. King instructed us to begin with this question, but not to reveal the answer until the very last sentence.

Jon did not have great social skills. What he did have was a hearing disorder. His hearing aids were not the almost invisible kind available today. On his belt, Jon wore a box, with wires from the box running under his shirt to a device in and behind his ear. The only time this contraption worked to Jon's advantage was when he would turn his hearing aid down or off and take a nap, right in front of the teacher.

Despite his disorder, Jon always wore a smile. We classmates did try to warm up to Jon. He was very friendly, although he talked funny. Because he could not hear well, it was difficult for him to form words the rest of us could understand. It was painfully difficult, both for Jon and for us.

The day the reports were due, Jon announced at first recess that he was going home with me after school. I had not invited him. At least, I didn't recall that I had. Jon was smiling from ear to ear as he made his declaration.

"Have you asked your mom?" I asked. (I know I hadn't asked my mother, which was a breach of our family's "Friend Etiquette.")

"Yeths," he replied exuberantly.

"How will you get home?"

He struggled to explain that he would go home with me after school, eat supper with my family—which was not acquainted with him—and ride to the baseball game with us. His mother would pick him up after we "slaughtered" the other team.

Jon and I played on the same Little League team. It is probably more accurate to say that I played and Jon watched. During the team warm-ups, Jon would throw with me. Most of my teammates ignored him. He was not very adept at throwing, and it was difficult to understand or converse with him. The coach was afraid to put him in, fearing he might get hurt due to his inability to hear. But Jon's mother wanted him to fit in, to belong.

When it was time to present the reports, Mrs. King called us up in alphabetical order. Jon's surname slated him last. As he moved to the front of the room, the class grew tense. How would Jon do? Would we be able to understand him? Whom would he pick as his best friend?

Jon struggled to shape words through his beaming smile. He could hardly wait to get to the last sentence so that he could proudly announce to the world who his best friend was. He was not nervous; he had practiced hard to stand before us.

The class understood about half of what Jon said, although it became clear that he would pick me. The entire length of his report he looked at me, at one point even smiling and pointing to me. He concluded "An myne est friend isth Gio Myerths."

That was years ago. I had questions then. I have questions now. How did this happen without my knowledge? How could I be his best friend? Did this mean he had to become mine?

+ *What Does It Mean to Belong?*

Belonging happens when you identify with another entity—a person or organization, or perhaps a species, culture, or ethnic group. Belonging need not be reciprocal. You can feel a sense of belonging—and in fact, can belong—without the other party's knowledge or sharing the experience. As we saw with Jon, belonging is an individual experience. He did not need my permission to belong to me in a significant way. To whom Jon belonged was under his control. To be sure, many of us have wanted to belong but have not been allowed "in." Had I told Jon I did not want to be his best friend, his experience of belonging would have changed.

Several years ago my wife and I began worshipping with a nearby congregation. We attended every weekend we were in town. We had been going there several months when a friendly lady smiled and said warmly, "It has been really nice to have you two popping in and out."

[Religious needs cannot be considered apart from the need
for community. People can and do move in and out of religious
traditions in search of meaningful community.[2]

**Mary Moore, quoted in "In Search of Belonging:
The Hispanic Religious Presence in Indianapolis"**]

Sara and I were surprised by the woman's assessment. We had thought we were coming "regularly." Sara and I were experiencing a wonderful sense of belonging—until the friendly lady, perhaps without intending to, let us know we were not following community rules. We did not yet belong.

There are many who consider themselves part of the community of faith until they are confronted by someone who tells them otherwise. Our culture wonders—with some confusion—"Why don't I belong?" And if there is one place that can welcome them with open arms, it is the church. In Jesus' story of the prodigal, the father welcomed his boy home by redefining what it meant to belong to the family.[3] Perhaps our definitions ought likewise to broaden.

+ *Finding Our Place in This World*

Tim grew up on the family farm, was the only one of the children to remain, and now owns the land and the buildings that represent so much of his life. His siblings are scattered about the world. Over the holidays the family returned, and Tim took a walk down the lane with his older sister, Pam. Their talk turned to reminiscing about old times and the journeys their lives had taken. Pam had traveled; Tim had not. Pam and her husband had shared several adventures; Tim had stayed home.

Tim expressed the feeling that his life had been a series of safe decisions. Pam was surprised. "But you take risks," she insisted. "Don't you worry about the crops? You plant and then pray that the right amount of rain will come and at the right time. Doesn't that worry you?"

"Oh, no," Tim answered quickly. "I don't worry about that."

Sensing he was not telling her everything, she probed. "What do you worry about?"

"I worry about being alone."

Being alone. This was something that never concerned most farmers of the past. The family stayed home. As life progressed, no one ever thought about being alone. The kids were given plots "on the back forty" to build a home and raise a family. When mom and dad could no longer work, the boys took over and cared for the land and the old folks as well.

Not so today. And this cultural shift is a major factor in our struggle to belong. People are trying to find their place in this world not in individualist ways but in ways that connect. They are searching for the "back forty," for a place to belong. They are searching for family.

Language and Belonging

Language may be the key element for developing and nurturing community. As people search for community, they are listening with their eyes, ears, and emotions. They are keenly aware of how we tell them they belong or don't belong.

It once seemed simpler. There were only two categories—members and nonmembers. Membership required contracts, beliefs, commitments, and rituals. There was a clearer line that determined when someone was "in." Now we struggle to build a community of believers in a culture that wants to experience belonging over believing.

People crave connection, not contracts. They want to participate in our rituals, even though they may not yet fully understand their meaning. They see a kaleidoscope of possibilities for belonging. But our language struggles to fully express this spectrum of possibilities.

[
The biggest challenge for the church at the opening of the twenty-first century is to develop a solution to the discontinuity and fragmentation of the American lifestyle.[4]

Lyle Schaller at a Leadership Network Conference
]

Rose Swetman describes what happened to Marilyn.

Marilyn is interested in investigating faith/spirituality and asked if she could attend church with her friend, Dee, who about 18 months prior decided to become a follower of Jesus through our church.

The second Sunday Marilyn attended church, the message was on the spiritual practices of fasting and prayer. We'd already decided that as a church we were going to participate in a community fast and prayer time for three days. After listening to the message and also being moved by the music that day, Marilyn told her friend she was going to fast with our community.

During the fast, Marilyn began reading *The Case for Christ* by Lee Strobel. We began our fast on a Thursday and ended on a Saturday evening. The following morning at church, Marilyn had not broken her fast. That morning there was a particular sweet presence of the Spirit among us. Again, Marilyn felt very moved by the music. She told me after, "I don't know what happened to me; the music so moved me all I could do was weep." She told Dee that while she was engaged with the music that morning she had made some important personal decisions. One decision was to try to reconnect with her father from whom she has been estranged for some time.

This is an amazing experience to witness and be a part of. People searching for faith, investigating spirituality, wanting to have an experience with God to the extent they would be involved in a community fast and prayer even before believing. I'm amazed and grateful of being able to just be who we are and invite others to join on our journey. While being sensitive to the Holy Spirit's work in their lives, we continue to invite them to follow Jesus.[5]

The writer Kathleen Norris reveals the ambiguity she felt in this area.

Whenever I filled out a form that requested my religious affiliation, I would write "nothing," aware that this wasn't quite true but having no language with which to address the truth. . . . If anything, it seemed unlikely to me that I would ever find a place for myself within the religious tradition of my inheritance. . . . When I first ventured back to Sunday worship in my small town, the services felt like a word bombardment, an hour-long barrage of heavyweight theological terminology. Often, I was so exhausted afterwards that I would need a three-hour nap. And I would wake depressed, convinced that this world called "Christian" was closed to me.[6]

We must discover the language that moves our definitions of community forward while at the same time give our culture a lexicon people can use to express their community experience. Our language needs to connect to an authentic piece of a person's community puzzle, so that when they see, hear, and feel our "words," they see, hear, and feel "welcome."

"Our task," according to Michael Ignatieff, "is to find a language for our need for belonging which is not just a way of expressing nostalgia, fear and estrangement from modernity."[7]

I remember an incident in my own life while I was serving a church in Tennessee. Very early one morning a nurse called to say that a Mrs. Peterson had passed away and that the family wanted me to come to the hospital. The congregation was small. (We had an attendance of thirty-five on Easter Sunday.) Most who attended were related. I called the elder. He did not know anyone named Mrs. Peterson. "She does not belong to us," he said confidently.

I went to the hospital wondering. The family greeted me as if I was an old friend. They said that Mother always mentioned how well the church had treated her. She had been grateful that she belonged to such a wonderful bunch of people.

The next day I checked the records. I checked with those who attended worship weekly. I checked with the old, old timers. No one knew Mrs. Peterson.

At the funeral I discovered that one of the members who had since died had regularly been "neighborly" to Mrs. Peterson. From those neighborly experiences, Mrs. Peterson felt like she belonged to the congregation in a profound way. She had found family.

In her last will and testament, she left the church a healthy sum of money. We were significant in her life. And even though Mrs. Peterson did not give a weekly commitment, she expressed generosity to us, her "family."

[
Atheism [Christianity] has been specially advanced through the loving service rendered to strangers, and through their care for the burial of the dead. It is a scandal that there is not a single Jew who is a beggar, and that the godless Galileans care not only for their own poor but for ours as well; while those who belong to us look in vain for the help that we should render them.[8]

Roman Emperor Julian
]

There are those who belong to our congregations who have not asked permission to do so. They connect with the congregation and they choose to belong. Sometimes they decide to follow our rules of engagement; at other times they create their own. Yet make no mistake; their experience of belonging is significant in their lives.

+ *Life's Fundamental Search*

On one occasion an expert in the law stood up to test Jesus. "Teacher," he asked, "what must I do to inherit eternal life?"

"What is written in the Law?" he replied. "How do you read it?"

He answered, "'Love the Lord your God with all your heart and with all your soul and with all your strength and with all your mind'; and, 'Love your neighbor as yourself.'"

"You have answered correctly," Jesus replied. "Do this and you will live."

But he wanted to justify himself, so he asked Jesus, "And who is my neighbor?"[9]

Who is my neighbor? Who belongs to me? To whom do I belong? For whom am I responsible—and to what extent? These are the timeless questions of the expert in the law.

"What must I do?" he asked. "Love God; love my neighbor?"

"Yes," Jesus replied.

The expert answered correctly. Why then did he not leave, satisfied that he had answered well the teacher's question? Beneath his belligerent façade, was he anxious about his own ability to love others? Did his adherence to the law leave him with an empty, limited definition of love? Of neighbor?

"Love your neighbor" was his answer. Was the law unclear in defining the neighborhood? Did this lie at the heart of the nagging cave deep within? Had he acquired purity, knowledge, and wisdom in the absence of community connection?

Why was the question, "Who is my neighbor?" a test? How are we to know who connects with us? How was I to know that my second-grade classmate, Jon, had become my neighbor? Why are we still tricked by this question?

The question "Who is my neighbor?" guides the church to its fundamental calling. And defining "neighborhood" has been one of the primary tasks for the church throughout its history. And in this postmodern, post-evangelical blip in time, we still struggle to guide people toward a healthy experience of community and belonging.

The search for community is a fundamental life search. We need to belong. We search with some increasing desperation as terms such as "neighbor," "family," and "congregation" are being redefined. People are searching to belong in new places and through new experiences.

"The Quest
for Community"

I want my community.

One of the favorite words used in the context of the Web is "community." eBay is in the business of building communities, they say; theirs is less an information source than a social medium.

The paradox is this: the pursuit of individualism has led us to this place of hunger for community, not of blood or nation but communities of choice.

More than buying and selling, the electronic emporium is about posting messages on bulletin boards, discovering new friends, and launching relationships at the eBay Cafe. One user said, "eBay is bringing people together to do a lot more than trading goods. We are trading our hearts."

Don't laugh.

eBay may just be the closest experience of small-town America available to postmoderns.[10]

Leonard Sweet, "The Quest for Community"

In the past, we have proposed that the answer could be found in Sunday school, in seeker worship, and/or in small groups. Some did find significant community in these programs, yet we are left bewildered, not always sure how it happens. Why do small groups work for some but not for others? Why do some seem to find fulfillment in public worship alone, without the aid of a "closer" church experience?

It seems that in many ways we are not helping people with their life search. Rather, we are merely supplying them with another numbing thing to do that masks the real, nagging ache of their search for a neighbor, for family, for belonging.

Elton Trueblood defines this investigation as a search for "bold fellowship": "Many contemporary seekers cannot abide the Church as they see it, their dissatisfaction arising not from the fact that membership demands too much, but rather from the fact that the demands are too small."[11]

I build on Trueblood's thoughts in this way: Christ's association included many persons who were not included in the fellowship of "the (institutional) church." The woman at the well, the tax collector in the inner circle, and a little man in a tree all found belonging. There was even room for a prostitute to join the family tree of the King. This is "bold fellowship." It is not found in the demands of membership but in the scope of who is allowed to belong and to experience family and home. "Who," not "What," is the essence of "love thy neighbor."

> Our relationship with each other is the criterion the world uses to judge whether our message is truthful—Christian community is the final apologetic.[12]
>
> **Francis Schaeffer**

In another story, Jesus had people asking, "Lord . . . when did we see you a stranger . . .?"[13] Who is allowed in our neighborhood? Who is a stranger? How we answer these questions goes a long way toward defining the church. And our culture is asking for new definitions of "church."

People are connecting in whatever places they are allowed to join in the journey. In the following chapters we will look at possibilities for whole, healthy community. Our journey will lead us to question established definitions. We will try to describe community experiences, not to prescribe them. This is a conversation, not a book of answers.

So disagree. Argue. Wrestle with the thoughts presented. And as the old paradigms of belonging change color when examined in the light, keep your own experiences at hand and see who belongs. Welcome to a new community conversation.

Now therefore ye are no more strangers and foreigners, but fellow citizens with the saints, and of the household of God.

Ephesians 2:19, KJV

+ [*consider*]

+ How do you define who belongs? Who fits in this definition and who does not?

+ Identify those who would say they belong but you do not consider "members" of "the family."

+ If you could redefine your membership, what would change? Who would change? You? Them?

+ Make a list of all the things you belong to, and consider how significant they are to your life. Does everyone (person, club, organization, informal connections) know you belong?

+ Have you ever been told you don't belong? What were the implications?

[*three*]

"give me some space"

People are strange when you're a stranger.[1]
Jim Morrison, "People Are Strange"

My wife and I were at the supermarket, playing the checkout game. You know it well; you've done it yourself. Glancing over the available lanes, I quickly calculated: fewest persons in line + fewest items in the carts ahead + alert and swift cashier + no blinking light above the register = the quickest line. We made our decision.

Sara by my side, our cart directly in front of us, I glanced over the point-of-purchase displays to see if we had indeed made a wise choice or if an early line withdrawal was needed. We were staying put. Sara rubbed my hand as if to say, "Well done." Then I caught a movement to my right. Just another shopper. *He's getting a pack of gum,* I thought. *Then he'll go back where he belongs—behind me.* Except he didn't. He stayed right next to me, almost blocking the narrow checkout lane.

I grew uncomfortable. Doesn't he know the rules? I gave him what I hoped was a polite but questioning look. It didn't work. Couldn't he take a hint? Now I was becoming aggravated. I began to sweat and fidget. *Stand behind me,* I thought, *not next to me.* My breathing rate increased. The room started to close in. I wanted him to move. Here was an unwelcome visitor in my space. An intruder. He did not belong there. I wanted to say to him, "Move to your own space."

+ *Communicating Belonging*

Have you ever tried to have a private conversation with a person standing on the other side of a crowded room? Or a large empty room? We may start our conversation in this space, but we quickly move closer.

Conversely, have you experienced the "too close talker"? Try to have a social conversation with someone who insists on invading your space. Your first reaction is to move away.

In the early 1960s, Edward T. Hall identified four spaces of human interaction: public, social, personal, and intimate. He assigned to each space a specific amount of real estate. According to Hall, in public space we stand twelve or more feet away from another person. In social space individuals stand four to twelve feet apart. In personal space, from eighteen inches to four feet; and in intimate space from actually touching to eighteen inches.[2]

Hall's findings form the backbone of proxemics, the study of how physical space influences culture and communication.[3] I have discovered that Hall's spaces are helpful categories not only for culture and communication, but also as they relate to community—our sense of belonging. We experience belonging in the same four spaces Hall describes: public, social, personal, and intimate.

How we occupy physical space—whether through actual real estate (the shopper standing next to my wife and me in the supermarket line) or through more subtle "spatial language"—tells others whether we want them to belong.

Spatial language refers to the words we use: *small* groups, *close* friends, *distant* relatives, *family* connections, *neighborly* attitudes. It also includes more subtle means; i.e., nonverbal communication. These accumulated messages communicate belonging (or the lack of belonging).

Let me illustrate:

Leah and Peter had been dating for several months. They had great fun together. Leah wanted to play matchmaker for her roommate, Jen. Peter thought Michael might be a good candidate.

So one Friday night Leah and Peter arranged for the four of them to meet at a restaurant and then see a movie. Conversation over dinner went well. Jen and Michael discovered they had a lot in common. On the way to the car and holding hands, Leah leaned up to Peter's ear and whispered, "What do you think?"

Peter shrugged. "Let's wait and see."

The movie, a comedy, offered many opportunities to laugh. Yet every time Leah peeked over at Jen, her arms were crossed. And her body was turned more toward Leah than Michael. *Hmmmm*, Leah thought.

After the movie, Jen was conversational, but she kept her hands in her pockets. When the time came for goodbyes, she thanked Michael for the evening, got into her car, and drove off.

"So, Michael," Leah asked, "Are you going to ask her out?"

He shook his head. "I don't think so."

Jen's manner was polite, but Michael had gotten the message.

+ *It's All in Your Head*

Our concept of space is largely a matter of perspective; it's in our minds. Humans adjust their definition of space based on surrounding variables. Animals do not seem to have this capacity. For most species, space is constant. For instance, a lion trainer knows that a lion will attack when a foe enters a specific and constant space. The trainer causes the lion to jump from platform to platform by invading this space. The trainer enters the space; the lion jumps. When he wants the lion to be still, the trainer moves away, and the lion remains in place.

By Hall's definition, a crowded elevator would be defined as intimate space. Passengers may be closer than Hall's eighteen inches; in fact they may be touching. To Hall, zero to eighteen inches is *intimate space*.

"What Contents of Space"

....

Space isn't empty; it is rich with meaning and plays a major role in shaping your relationships.

People ... carry about with them mobile personal territories which only those "close" to them are welcome to enter. Generally speaking, this personal airspace is coffin-shaped, extending three to five feet in front for strangers, one and one-half to three feet for friends, and much less on the back and sides. If you come closer, you are signaling a desire to be either hostile or intimate. If you stay farther away, you're "saying" you are aware of their presence, but aren't really interested in making contact. . . .

If someone seems uncomfortable around you, the problem may not lie in the topic, your breath, or your personal style. The problem may simply be that you are standing too close.

A plumbing contractor complained to me that both his customers and his neighbors seemed edgy around him and backed away whenever he talked to them. When he tried to reestablish what he felt was a comfortable distance, they would back away again and it sometimes seemed as though he was chasing them around the room. He added that washing his mouth five times daily with Listerine hadn't helped in the least.

I suggested to this gentleman, as I backed into my desk in a futile attempt to get farther away, that what he considered a comfortable distance for social and business exchanges was, to many others including myself, an intimate distance. With coaching, he learned to place himself four feet away and then let others decide where to stand.[4]

Alan Garner, *Conversationally Speaking*

But we know differently. Even though we are very close in terms of real estate, mentally we massage the space into *public space*. We may be touching yet we are far from intimate.

We humans manipulate space all the time. In our minds. This mixture of physical space plus mental exercise helps us interpret how—or if—we belong and how—or if—we experience community.

+ *The Four Spaces*

Some connections take place spontaneously. (This concept will be developed in chapter 4, Group Chemistry.) Some connections fulfill a need at a specific time in our lives. (More on this in chapter 5, Trading Spaces.)

But in all four spaces:
+ We connect.
+ We are committed and participate.
+ We find the connection significant.

Public Space

I love new technologies, and I am an early adopter. Recently when I had to replace my cell phone, I selected a model that had been released only a few days before. The day after I made my purchase, a waitress came over and asked me how I liked the phone. She, too, had just bought one and was "in love with it."

[Upoc members can set up groups in any of three ways—secret, private, or public. Anyone can join a public group. Private groups are listed in the directory, but people join by applying and can be expelled by the founder. Secret groups are not listed and are known only to their members.[5]

Howard Rheingold, *Smart Mobs: The Next Social Revolution*]

Later that same day a teenager at the mall spotted my phone and bolted over to see the new "rad" model. I find this kind of community around most of the toys I purchase. There is a mobile phone

community. There is a Palm® community. There is a Macintosh®
community. Most, if not all, are public spatial communities.

John Johnston describes another public community:

> They arrive more than an hour early, many of them. They
> buy their game sheets, stake out a favorite spot, settle in and
> wait for Doug Robinson, the caller, to say: "I want to welcome
> everybody to St. Boniface Thursday night bingo."
> And then, "Your first number: I-29."
> By that time—shortly after 7 p.m.—the St. Boniface
> School cafeteria in Northside is packed with nearly 200 peo-
> ple—mostly women—eager to blot out bingo numbers with
> ink daubers.
> Some players come from the immediate neighborhood.
> Some drive or bus from miles away. Some come to be with fam-
> ily. Some come to get away from family. Some come to
> unwind.[6]

On one level it's all about lining up five numbers and yelling
"Bingo!" Yet this is not only about playing a game and winning a few
bucks. These people come week after week, month after month, and
year after year to connect with others in a public space that is significant for them.

Some theorists suggest that it is impossible to make significant
connections in public spaces. Don't tell these people that. Their connections burrow deep. I doubt that they visit each other's homes or
get together outside of the bingo hall, yet they care for one another—
all in public space. They may not know each other's names, but they
are not strangers. They are family.

Rabbi Jennifer Krause shares an anecdote illustrating how powerful and meaningful public acquaintances can be. In the *Newsweek*
article "The Ones Who Turn Up Along the Way," she recounts stories
of her acquaintance with Walter, her building super, and Ali, the
manager of her neighborhood grocery.

> I share these stories because they are part of the puzzle of
> community. I am well aware that Walter and Ali do not fall into
> the simple categories of family member, co-worker or friend.
> We are from different backgrounds, different countries, and we
> occupy different socioeconomic spheres. We don't go to each
> other's home for dinner or make plans to meet for coffee, and
> we probably won't. Our connections are site-specific and
> episodic. And yet they make real claims on my heart and mind.[7]

Rabbi Krause seems surprised that despite her "site-specific and episodic" relationships with Walter and Ali, her limited contact with them has grown to mean something to her. Should we be surprised that mere acquaintances (public space) can hold significance in one's "heart and mind"?

Unlike Rabbi Krause, all too often we are not content to leave these one-time, site-specific, episodic relationships alone. We push and pull, trying to move these relationships to the next level. This is not helpful, and may be unhealthy. For harmony and for the sake of health, we need significant belonging in all four spaces: public, social, personal, and intimate.

In fact, public belonging is a space where we need numerous significant relationships in order to experience a sense of healthy belonging and community. We need to develop *more* connections in this space than in any of the other three.

A Valid Public Stand. I am a member in good standing of The Grand Old Party. Yet the only indication that I am a Republican is that I show up and vote. I do not stuff envelopes or attend party events. I do not ask others to contribute money. I have never campaigned for office. I belong to the party only in public space.

The party accepts this fact. They never suggest that if I really want to belong I will need to become more committed. They never hint that if I were to come closer to the organization I would be a more authentic Republican. They validate *my space of belonging.*

In the 2000 presidential election, Florida could not tell immediately who would receive the electoral vote. During the controversy, I (and other public belongers to both parties) became more involved. When the "family" is in trouble, those accepted as family come to the family's—or party's—aid.

Public belonging happens when we connect through outside influences. It isn't about connecting person to person; it is about sharing a common experience. Think of fans at a football game, members of the PTA, shoppers at a grocery store. In each case an outside influence brings these people into a common grouping. They connect because of the outside influence, not because of shared personal information.

If they were to exchange personal information they, by definition, move to a different space.

Public Space: Only for Strangers? There is a difference between *stranger* and *public belonger*. The stranger does not feel connected. The public belonger does. The "stranger" who connects has moved to "public belonger." The belonging, however, does not have to be mutual. It is more about how it feels to the person and less about how the organization views him.

> In *Rational Ritual: Culture, Coordination, and Common Knowledge*, Michael Suk-Young Chwe claims that public rituals are "social practices that generate common knowledge," which enables groups to solve coordination problems. Suk-Young Chwe writes: "A public ritual is not just about the transmission of meaning from a central source to each member of an audience; it is also about letting audience members know what other audience members know."[8]
>
> **Michael Suk-Young Chwe, Rational Ritual: Culture, Coordination, and Common Knowledge**

We often equate "stranger" with "anonymous." If we don't know someone's name, we consider that person a stranger. Yet when I shared "high-fives" with nameless fans around me after our Hoosiers sank the winning basket, I certainly did not feel like a stranger. Nor did they. We belonged to the same team. We connected.

As modern and hypermodern churches grew, they embraced anonymity for first-time guests: "Let somebody explore the faith without any level of commitment. Let's see what happens," they said, thus providing a comfortable public space for visitors. Or so they thought. People may want anonymity, but they do not want to be strangers. They do not want to be strangers to the communication styles. They do not want to be strangers to the décor, the music, the language, even the inside jokes. They came to church wanting to connect with God, and they certainly do not want us to make them feel like they are strangers to him.

Public Belongers Are Committed and Participate. We tend to validate only those ways in which we want people to participate. In truth, people participate in many ways.

I mentioned the Hoosiers earlier. I am a huge Indiana University men's basketball fan. I belong to the team publicly. To them I may be nameless, but I'm not a stranger. I've adjusted my schedule to see games, both in person and on TV. I buy a special cable package to see games not broadcast on regular TV or standard cable. I wear official IU garb. I'm not hesitant about praising or arguing in favor of the team. I am a committed public belonger.

It is simply not true that people who belong only in public space are "on the fringe." Nor is it true that we somehow need to get them to move "closer" to get them to be committed.

Were we to validate the space people inhabit—whichever of the four spaces it may be—we will find countless people who are actively committed, who are happy to participate, and who have previously been eased aside into the shadows or written off entirely.

Public spatial belonging is not about anonymity. And anonymity has little to do with commitment. People can—and do—experience connectedness at different levels, and when they feel connected, they explore the possibilities of significant, committed participation.

Consider Jesus' encounter with the soldier, a centurion in the Roman army of occupation.

> When Jesus had entered Capernaum, a centurion came to him, asking for help. "Lord," he said, "my servant lies at home paralyzed and in terrible suffering."
>
> Jesus said to him, "I will go and heal him."
>
> The centurion replied, "Lord, I do not deserve to have you come under my roof. But just say the word, and my servant will be healed. For I myself am a man under authority, with soldiers under me. I tell this one, 'Go,' and he goes; and that one, 'Come,' and he comes. I say to my servant, 'Do this,' and he does it."
>
> When Jesus heard this, he was astonished and said to those following him, "I tell you the truth, I have not found anyone in Israel with such great faith. I say to you that many will come from the east and the west, and will take their places at the feast with Abraham, Isaac and Jacob in the kingdom of heaven. But the subjects of the kingdom will be thrown outside, into the darkness, where there will be weeping and gnashing of teeth."

Then Jesus said to the centurion, "Go! It will be done just as you believed it would." And his servant was healed at that very hour.[9]

Jesus is a master at permitting people to belong to him in all four spaces. He offered to come to the centurion's home. Why didn't the centurion want Jesus to come? He had his reasons. Matthew says he felt he did not deserve it. Luke says the centurion did not consider himself worthy.

Whatever the reason, Jesus accepted the centurion's statement; he did not insist on coming closer. He allowed this centurion to be a part of the "family" in public space. The centurion did not want to be intimate with Jesus. The centurion was not after a personal or a social relationship. He needed Jesus to accept him in a public space and yet help in a significant way. Jesus honored that request.

True community can be experienced in public space. Public space is not mere togetherness; it is connectedness. It is *family*. An essential key to developing community is the maturing of our competencies for growing significant, committed public belongings.

What would this look like in our congregations? Can we be comfortable with people belonging to Jesus and the church in *public space*? Can we give them help, hope, and home in the space where they choose to belong? Without pushing them to come closer?

Social Space

Several years ago, I was the lead teacher for a Sunday morning class of adults, couples in their twenties and thirties. We began each class period with donuts and coffee. To me it seemed like half the class time was spent on social activity.

At least once a month we got together during the week to "have some fun." The church grew, and so did the class.

After several months I began to become dissatisfied with the spiritual and relational growth of the group. I was sure it was my responsibility to lead us into "a deeper relationship with God and each other," so I planned a lengthy study and gathered material. Things went well. Everyone enjoyed the topic, and new faces showed up with regularity. I felt a great sense of accomplishment.

We came to the last session, for which I had designed a Sunday of Commitment. We were going to spend the entire hour discussing the next steps, ending in a time where everyone would commit to the practices we studied.

To give a different and "serious" feel to the morning, I determined that we would skip the refreshments. However, as the first couples arrived, seeing the absence of food they went roaming through other classrooms searching to find extras to fill the void.

As I started our journey through the hour of commitment, I could see that for the first time I was losing their attention. I spoke more firmly. They pushed farther away. When it came time to sign on the dotted line, they had mentally escaped to a safe place.

My wife and I had a long discussion that week. I was very discouraged. Our indictment was, "All they want is to socialize." I said to her, "If they want to remain so self-centered and shallow, I can no longer be the teacher." She agreed. The next week I quit.

The class grew and grew up. They became parents. Some relocated with new job opportunities. Yet the group dynamic never changed: They related to each other socially. In *social space*.

I have grown up, too. I am now aware that those in the class *needed* to connect socially. There was nothing superficial about the relationships. The relationships were significant and shaped the growth of many.

Recently I met one of the class members for lunch. We've kept in touch and consider each other friends. When we get together, the discussion always goes back to the Sunday mornings when we met for donuts. Listening to our discussions, it is obvious that those relationships were significant to both of us. Those "shallow" Sundays had shaped our lives.

In many ways, social belonging is the "small talk" of our relationships. We denigrate social belonging as superficial. We surmise that nothing significant takes place in social relationships.

However,

> If you don't think much of small talk, try living without it for a while. One of the chief complaints of those in so-called commuter marriages is the inability to discuss the inane. One commuter wife observed that "you have a lot of immediate

impressions and little jokes and observations that you can't save for a week. You can't reconstruct that kind of trivia in an effective way. I find the loss of that material really annoying." Another geographically displaced wife lamented lost opportunities "to share in everyday things like 'What did you have for lunch today?'"[10]

Take away social relationships and our *community conversation* becomes flat, lacking a spontaneous connection to the entirety of our relationships.

Three Factors in Social Belonging. Social belonging is the space where we connect through sharing "snapshots" of who we are. Such phrases as "first impression" and "best foot forward" refer to this type of spatial belonging.

Social belonging is important for three reasons. First, it provides space for *neighbor relationships*. It used to be that neighbor meant "friend." Now when we say neighbor, it doesn't necessarily mean friend. It could mean someone who lives geographically close. If I have a neighbor who is a friend, I usually say exactly that, "I have a neighbor who is a friend."

A neighbor is someone you know well enough to ask for small favors—to walk the dog or pick up the mail. We meet briefly on the way out the door or during an evening walk. These relationships bring to a neighborhood safety, comfort, and connectedness.

Second, this social space provides a safe selection space for us to decide with whom we would like to grow a "deeper" relationship. In social space we present information that enables others to decide whether or not they connect with us. In return, we get just enough information to decide whether to keep this person in this space or to move him or her to another space.

Third, these interactions allow us to display a reality we create of who we are, while at the same time enabling others to "witness a sample of the process through which this reality was created over the months and years."[11] This helps others with their own process of self-discovery and definition.

I have a solid sense of self. However, many times I stumble in social settings, especially at the beginning. One reason is that I have a number of ways to describe "me." I am a partner in a publishing services firm. I am a consultant. I am a husband and father. I am an artist. I write. I teach. I speak to large groups. I sometimes serve as a pastor.

When someone asks me, "So, what do you do?" I consider who is asking and quickly assess the surrounding company and circumstances. When asked that question, I silently ask another question of myself: "What image makes the most sense for this person to see me as?" Then I try to match an accurate definition of "me" to the situation so that my answer connects to the person asking.

Sharing an authentic definition of who you are helps make significant social connections. Your definition of who you are helps you and helps the other person to connect, thus nurturing an experience of belonging for both of you.

Personal Belonging

I enjoyed high school, mostly for the relationships that developed during those four years. Even today, twenty-plus years afterward, I list Grant as one of the very few "best friends" I have had in my life.

Grant and I were always there for each other. We synchronized our class schedules, spent every lunch hour at the same cafeteria table, shared our "wisdom" about the world, and found weekend jobs where we could work as a team. Together we did a lot of good, and we also got into a lot of mischief.

I moved to Tennessee to go to college. Grant moved to Michigan. Our paths rarely crossed. Yet on one rare occasion when Grant and I happened to be home over the same weekend, it was as if we had never been apart. We picked up right where we had left off.

When I think of personal spatial connections, I think of connections such as the one I have with Grant. Even now—after all these years—we share private information. Both of us know that this information is in safekeeping.

Personal space is where we connect through sharing private—although not "naked"—experiences, feelings, and thoughts.

"*Social and Civic History*"

We were a "can do" people, who accomplished whatever we set out to do. We had licked the Depression, turned the tide in World War II, and rebuilt Europe after the war. . . . Freedom Summer was an audacious undertaking consistent with the exaggerated sense of importance and potency shared by the privileged members of America's postwar generation.

The baby boom meant that America's population was unusually young, whereas civic involvement generally doesn't bloom until middle age. In the short run, therefore, our youthful demography actually tended to dampen the ebullience of civil society. But that very bulge at the bottom of the nation's demographic pyramid boded well for the future of community organizations, for they could look forward to swelling membership rolls in the 1980s, when the boomers would reach the peak "joining" years of the life cycle. And in the meantime, the bull session buzz about "participatory democracy" and "all power to the people" seemed to augur ever more widespread engagement in community affairs. One of America's most acute social observers prophesied in 1968, "Participatory democracy has all along been the political style (if not the slogan) of the American middle and upper class. It will become a more widespread style as more persons enter into those classes." Never in our history had the future of civic life looked brighter.

What happened next to civic and social life in American communities is the subject of [*Bowling Alone*]. In recent years social scientists have framed concerns about the changing character of American society in terms of the concept of "social capital." By analogy with notions of physical capital and human capital—tools and training that enhance individual productivity—the core idea of social capital theory is that social networks have value. Just as a screwdriver (physical capital) or a college education (human capital) can increase productivity (both individual and collective), so too social contacts affect the productivity of individuals and groups.

Whereas physical capital refers to physical objects and human capital refers to properties of individuals, social capital refers to connections among individuals—social networks and the norms of reciprocity and trustworthiness that arise from them. In that sense social capital is closely related to what some have called "civic virtue." The difference is that "social capital" calls attention to the fact that civic virtue is most powerful when embedded in a dense network of reciprocal social relations. A society of many virtuous but isolated individuals is not necessarily rich in social capital.

[T]hose tangible substances [that] count for most in the daily lives of people: namely good will, fellowship, sympathy, and social intercourse among the individuals and families who make up a social unit. . . . The individual is helpless socially, if left to himself. . . . If he comes into contact with his neighbor, and they with other neighbors, there will be an accumulation of social capital, which may immediately satisfy his social needs and which may bear a social potentiality sufficient to the substantial improvement of living conditions in the whole community. The community as a whole will benefit by the cooperation of all its parts, while the individual will find in associations the advantages of the help, the sympathy, and the fellowship of his neighbors.[12]

Robert D. Putnam, *Bowling Alone: The Collapse and Revival of American Community*

We call the people we connect with in this space "close friends." These are those who know more about us than an acquaintance would know and yet not so much that they feel uncomfortable.

These are the relationships most people mention when they think of "community." These connections are their models for "community."

These are also the relationships many call "intimate," which has led to much confusion. The problem is that when I define my personal relationships as *intimate*, I dilute the meaning of those relationships I hold in truly intimate space.

> The idea is this: When two people connect, when their beings intersect as closely as two bodies during intercourse, something is poured out of one and into the other that has the power to heal the soul of its deepest wounds and restore it to health.…
> But it rarely happens.[13]
>
> **Larry Crabb, Connecting: Healing for Ourselves and Our Relationships: A Radical New Vision**

For example, were I to define my relationship with Grant as "intimate," what term would be left to describe my relationship with my wife? I don't share the same kind of information with Grant as I do with Sara. Nor do I share information in the same way as I do with my Sara.

The two relationships are not the same. I take care of these two relationships in two different ways. When we describe personal relationships as intimate relationships, we confuse people's definitions and actions.

Intimate Belonging

In intimate space, we share "naked" experiences, feelings, and thoughts. Very few relationships are intimate. Intimate relationships are those in which another person knows the "naked truth" about us and yet the two of us are "not ashamed."

Eden was created in perfection. God fashioned all relationships to operate in perfect harmony. The intimate relationship was described as "naked and not ashamed." When this harmony was broken the intimate relationship suffered, as did all other relationships.[14]

Intimacy is based on the definitions of "nakedness" and "ashamed." Nakedness is not only physical. It is also emotional, informational, and spatial. Consider for example the examinations of a gynecologist or a urologist. Touching a person's genitals would usually be described as intimate. However, there are great measures taken to keep this experience public.

> The major definition to be sustained for this purpose is "this is a medical situation" (not a party, sexual assault, psychological experiment, or anything else). If it is a medical situation, then it follows that "no one is embarrassed" and "no one is thinking in sexual terms." Anyone who indicates to the contrary must be swayed by some nonmedical definition.[15]

"Ashamed" does not mean embarrassed. Embarrassment does not necessarily include shame. Shame is the experience of the intimate self exposed in an inappropriate space.

We tend to think of intimacy as the "Mecca" of relationship. But would all relationships be better if they were intimate? Think of all the relationships in your life, from bank teller to sister to coworker to spouse. Could we even adequately sustain all these relationships if they were intimate?

+ Healthy Community

All belonging is significant. Healthy community—the goal humankind has sought since the beginning—is achieved when we hold harmonious connections within all four spaces. Harmony means more public belongings than social. More social than personal. And very few intimate.

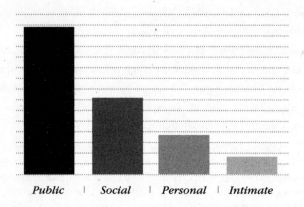

Public | Social | Personal | Intimate

A healthy strategy for those working to build community entails allowing people to grow significant relationships in all four spaces— *all four*. It means permitting people to belong in the space they want or need to belong. Insisting that real, authentic, true community happens only when people get "close" is a synthetic view of reality and may actually be harmful.

Kennon Callahan suggests that the "search for community is the search for roots, place, and belonging. It is the search for sharing and caring, for family and friends."[16] Not everyone wants his or her "place" to be an intimate one. Nor is that even possible. Announcing programs that promise intimacy to every person within reach creates unrealistic expectations. Worse, it actually pushes those who are not ready for such relationships farther away.

Community, *true* community, can and does deliver roots, place, and belonging. But it delivers these relationships in the particular space occupied by the particular person at that particular time. True community is accomplished through the significant relationships we embrace in all four spaces.

On a recent trip to Oregon, I sat with a couple of friends in one of Portland's tiny neighborhood diners. The food and service were good, and the atmosphere was true to the clientele. Karen, the manager, is a young woman in her twenties full of hopes and dreams. Making her rounds, she stopped at our table with more than the usual, "How is your meal—can I get you anything?"

In a very pleasant and appealing way she wanted to know who we were and what had brought us to her place. She had noticed our intense conversation, so she asked us what was so interesting. We were glad to share some "snapshots." Then Karen shared one of her own, telling us that she hoped to move to Nashville soon and open a restaurant in partnership with her best friend. "I don't much like Portland," she told us. "It is not a very friendly city. I mean, it's like this: People on the street say 'Hi' and everything, but they don't mean it." She went on, "When I go to parties or hang out in clubs, all I see are these little cliques everywhere. I can't find anyone I can get really close to."

Karen is not alone in her search. This is the cry of many. But how do we help?

> Maybe "going to church," more than anything else, means relating to several people in your life differently.[17]
>
> **Larry Crabb, Connecting: Healing for Ourselves and Our Relationships: A Radical New Vision**

An instinctive response might be to help Karen make more contacts. Or to help her meet a different set of people. However, Karen does not struggle with contacts. She greets people on the street, hangs out at clubs, and certainly found no problem engaging our table in conversation.

Yet in some significant way these contacts do not fulfill her search to belong. We might be tempted to rush to her ending statement—"I can't find anyone I can get really close to"—and try to find someone with interests similar to hers, about the same age, the same social status. Or we might try to engage Karen personally: She could be *our* friend.

Her statement is both interesting and confusing, especially considering what she told us about her friend. Over and over she expressed how close they are, adding several interesting vignettes that showed a table of strangers the truth of her words. So what is she searching for? More "close friends"?

Karen's experience is not uncommon. We all have some significant connections. We go to parties, enjoy long conversations with friends, talk to our neighbors, visit with our families. Yet we struggle to feel a whole, healthy sense of community. We don't feel as connected as we want to be. Something is missing.

Might this confusion come because we've been told often that we can experience community only in the "right" way? Is it because the experts try to get us to develop all or most of our relationships in personal or intimate space?

Again, true community is built in *four spaces:* public, social, personal, and intimate. As we help people with their lives, we need to allow them to live in the spaces they choose. We can encourage them to belong in the space that is comfortable for them at the time, treating them as a significant part of the "family" in whichever space they choose.

Be at peace. People connect and are motivated to connect in all four spaces. It is our charge to invite the stranger in. We do not invite strangers in for intimacy. We invite them in so they will no longer be strangers. We give space and they find family, belonging, and community. So gently knock and wait for them to invite you into the space where they are.

+ *"A Selling Space"*

On a recent out-of-town trip, I walked into a GNC store, looking for some vitamins. The moment I entered, a voice from the back of the store greeted me: "How's it goin'?"

"Doing well," I replied.

Not missing a beat, I began my search. By now the voice was a person and coming closer. I did not make eye contact and did not want to. In the back of my mind I knew the greeting was entirely too jolly for the salesperson to let our conversation end.

He let me search for a few seconds, and then interrupted the silence with, "Can I help you find something?"

My reaction was a quick, "No, thank you. I'm just looking." There; I had done it. I had brushed him off.

My reply to him was not quite the truth. I wasn't just browsing to see what was available; I was looking for something specific. A few more seconds passed as I went into "hunter-gatherer" mode, scanning the shelves for the container's familiar size, color, and design. Thank God for franchising. You can count on the franchise, from city to city, to shelve product in approximately the same place. I went to my right, stopping in mid-store. There it is. *Grab it and go*, I said to myself.

Just as I reached for the item I noticed a similar formula to its left. "I have a couple of customers who swear by that one," the sales-man said, moving closer. I did not respond. I didn't want his input. I knew what I wanted. *Get it and go*, I shouted to myself.

Still only a few steps away he started spouting a laundry list of nutritional information. He kept talking: "You need to—You should supplement this with that—" He kept piling information all over me.

"I'll just get this," I said, moving toward the checkout counter.

"Great! Have you tried—?"

I reminded him, "No, I think this will be all."

Following me to the checkout, he continued to engage me as he rang up my two items. "Do you have one of our Gold Member cards?" "No, and I don't think I want one tonight. Thanks."

"You're not from here, are you?"

"No," I told him. "I'm from Cincinnati."

"What brings you to these parts?"

"I am writing a book, and I thought—"

He did not let me finish. "You're writing a book? What's it about?"

This question, and his enthusiasm, slowed my exit strategy. "It's about how we communicate space to help people connect, belong, and develop community," I told him.

"Hey, that's cool," he responded. "Tell me more. What do you mean 'communicate space'?"

"People want to connect," I said, and proceeded to share with him. "All of us have a need to belong. Belonging happens in four spaces: public, social, personal, and intimate. When we recognize that people have different spaces they want to connect with us in, we can match our communication tools to the context and help them feel safe and comfortable. When we speak a spatially foreign vocabulary, they feel uneasy, anxious."

"Wow," he said. "That's real cool. But how does all this relate to someone like me?"

"Well," I began, "you asked me if I wanted a membership card, right? Do you know why I didn't want the card?"

"No," he responded, "but there are people who say 'No' and they come in here all the time. They could really save a lot of cash. It's a good deal."

I decided to level with him. "I didn't want the card because I don't want to be that close to you. I don't want you to send me mail. I don't want you to have all my personal information in your database. It is simply too close."

"I can see that," he told me. "You really fought me as I was trying to help. I was getting too close, wasn't I?"

"Yes. You see, people come here to buy personal items. Sometimes, intimate items. People come to find help with their weight. Others come because of an illness or the fear of illness."

He interrupted again: "And some come for help with their sex life."

"That's right," I agreed. "You are neither a grocery store nor a department store. You sell personal and intimate product, much like Victoria's Secret. People are cold to you when you invade their space with an inappropriate sales model."

"So how do I develop a sales model that helps them feel comfortable?" he asked.

"I'm not sure," I told him, "but I think most people like the opportunity to choose what space and how they would like to experience the sale and purchase of these items. Maybe the model looks like a gentle knock to let people know you are here if they need you, then step back and let them open the door."

"Yes, that's it. Like with you, I invaded your space, which was not good. However, I finally knocked in a way that you opened up. It's all about giving people the space to decide how they want to belong to this store and product." He thought a moment, then added, "Wow; that's cool, a selling space."

+ [*consider*]

+ How many public belongers connect with you and your congregation? What would happen if their experience of belonging would be counted as significant? What could they do to show their commitment?

+ What would it look like to provide spaces for social interaction? Can you provide these spaces without any hidden agendas to move people to another space?

+ Consider spending a week logging all of your spatial connections. What would happen if one or more of those spaces disappeared? What would happen if all of the people connected in one space decided to move to another?

+ What does it mean to be "transparent" in each of the four spaces? Is it different for each space?

+ Is there a space where you or your congregation are excessive in providing significant belonging? Is there a space in which you are deficient?

+ Do you trust people enough to allow them to belong in the space they choose?

four

group chemistry

Today, the most fascinating and pressing problems almost invariably center on efforts to unravel the delicate and intricate organization of networks of bewildering complexity.[1]

Mark Buchanan, *Nexus: Small Worlds and the Groundbreaking Science of Networks*

"It's not working," he moaned. "I have one of the most respected and most imitated small group programs in the country and I'm here to confess—it doesn't work."

I wasn't surprised. Nor were any of the others sitting around the table. There were twenty pastors and key leaders gathered that day, and I'm sure every one of us was glad that Jim had found the strength to express the truth so honestly.

I had been invited to participate in this meeting of small group leaders. Although I was not "one of them," the conference sponsor thought I might have some insights to share and some knowledge to gain. We spent half the first day building rapport. Yes, there were the usual "icebreaker" games. After all, wasn't this a forum on building effective small groups for the emerging culture?

Finally the games ended and the talk turned to small groups. Our facilitator asked each of us to express what we believed to be the three leading questions facing small group ministry. Each person offered well-considered questions, which were received with nods and murmurs of affirmation.

Because no one knew me, I was last to respond:

1. Does everyone need to be in a small group to experience significant, healthy community?
2. Do small groups help or hinder a person's search to belong?
3. Are small groups honestly the most significant way a person can grow in relationship to others and to God?

The facilitator stood silent for a few seconds. Astonished stares came from wide-eyed pastors. It seemed as if everyone was holding their breath. I was sure that what was to follow would be unfriendly. Finally, someone broke the silence: "Of course. Of course not. And of course. Next." The group broke into laughter, all of us knowing it was not this simple.

It took the remainder of the conference to unwrap what happened next. The most respected of the small group pastors in attendance confessed, "My small groups don't really work. They never have. To be honest, I don't think they're for everyone. In fact, I have never attended a small group nor wanted to attend one."

It was at this point when Jim made his comment. Others followed. Before long, everyone seemed to agree that small groups could be helpful, but they do not guarantee community.

Our discussion set us to wondering along the following lines:

+ How do we create a genuine experience of belonging?
+ How can we help people grow in a way or in ways that help them connect and experience community?
+ Why are some of the groups we create so empty?
+ Why do some of our groups seem forced?

Does any of this sound familiar?

Pete describes how he sees it:

> I finally blew the whistle. I rushed into staff meeting and announced that the small group ministry was coming to a halt. I can no longer try to massage something to life. It's over. We are not helping people feel like they belong. Only a small percentage of the groups we start actually help. All the other groups suck the energy right out of the leaders we've trained. We have a high level of leader burnout because of this. Until we find out what really helps people grow and experience community, it's over.

Gabe adds his perspective:

> It's a farce. I've read all the books. I've attended all the suggested conferences. I've followed the models to the nth degree, and yet nothing really works well. The killer is that I am worn to the bone. I believe that they should work. I know people need help and seek a real hope to belong. I even believe they have some biblical truth behind them. So why don't they work?

Some of the stories people have shared with me have been expressions of "failure," such as those above. Others have been stories of success. What makes the difference? As I've worked with pastors and key leaders across the country, some insights have emerged:

+ Small groups are not necessarily the most significant way to help people grow in relationship to God and to one another.

+ People connect in all four spaces, not in just one or two.

+ Community happens spontaneously.

+ We can facilitate environments that help people connect.

+ *Small Groups Are Not the Only Way*

> Who started this theory of "building community through small group" thing anyway? I would like to find them and wring their neck.
> I was given the responsibility to start and run small groups in our church after my senior pastor returned from a conference where he was told, "If you want to grow, you need small groups." What kind of foundation is that for pushing people into another once-a-week meeting?
> I am questioned monthly now about how many small groups we presently have. My evaluation is connected directly to this number and my success is dependent on it. If people don't like small groups, it is because I'm doing something wrong. If the congregation is not adding to its numbers, I must be doing something wrong.
> How could something this important be based upon material that is thrown together with little thought as to what the purpose is? Can anyone tell me why we spend so much energy on a house with little or no foundation?

These are good questions. Why *do* we promote small groups as the most significant way to build community and congregation? Why *have* they become a fad of our time? Why *do* we lead our congregants to believe that small groups deliver the community they seek?

Some congregations went to small groups hoping to increase attendance. Remember the *felt-need* groups? "If we can just get them into the building, maybe some of them will stay" was the pervasive thought. Others started small groups in order to grow people into "fully devoted followers of Christ," whatever that means.

Reasons for starting small groups usually included the words "to grow community" or "to help people belong." Have you ever said, "We have small groups because as the congregation grows larger we must grow smaller?"

Unwittingly we have promoted two exclusive environments of belonging—large (public) and small (intimate). This does not lead to healthy belonging.

+ *Connecting in All Four Spaces*

When people share stories about how they connect with others in significant ways they reveal that:

+ they want help with their lives,
+ they have a deep longing to belong, and
+ they seek to connect in spontaneous and healthy ways.

Having visited a number of congregations, I am aware that most of them offer opportunities for community in all four spaces: public, social, personal, and intimate. Yet almost all of them, including my own, have adopted a pattern of teaching attendees only two ways of belonging: public and intimate.

Public belonging is evident when we worship together, pray together, greet each other, laugh together, and share announcements that apply to the whole group, not just to a select few. We invite people to gather as one.

We may also communicate to people that they *don't* belong publicly. For example, we may "dis-invite" visitors or first-time attendees to contribute financially. It's the "in thing" to say, "Don't feel compelled to put anything in the offering when the plate passes by you. Those who call this congregation 'home' use this as a time of giving back to God a portion of the blessings he's brought to us."

Yes, this may make some of our guests feel relaxed. But we may also be teaching them that:

1. We have a special relationship with God. He has blessed us.
2. You don't. He has not yet blessed you. You must belong in a different way (space) to receive this blessing.

Similarly, we emphasize the intimate space of belonging to God. Prayer is taught as being a private conversation with God. Discipleship is represented as a one-on-one relationship with a person who knows God in a deeper way than you do. Or we say, "If you really want to know what our church is about, you need to get involved in a small group."

Again, human beings communicate and develop a sense of belonging in all four spaces. All four spaces are where we connect, grow roots, and satisfy our search for community. And harmony among the spaces—all four of them—builds healthy community in individuals and organizations.

Notice that I am not saying that we must process people from public to social to personal to intimate.

Notice that I am not saying that "intimate" is our ultimate goal. Intimate is not the most important, the most real, or the most authentic relationship.

The secret is to see *all* connections as significant. All of these spaces are important, real, and authentic in people's lives. We need to validate what people themselves count as valid. When we validate the space where they are, we greatly increase our ability to bring help to their lives.

+ *Spatially Specific Competencies*

Some competencies are general while others are spatially specific. General competencies are the foundation upon which the spatially specific competencies are built.

The general competencies enable people to move through life easily, connecting where they want to connect and belonging where they want to belong. Those who have a healthy sense of the general competencies:

+ have solid self-esteem,
+ possess flexible and effective communication skills,
+ live with a sense of fun.

Spatially specific competencies are discovered as people move from space to space, as people build a healthy knowledge of who they are, and as people recognize and follow accepted forms of behavior within a particular space. Each space requires its own set of competencies. A person might be fully competent in one space, but totally incompetent in another. As people build these competencies, they will increase their ability to hold significant, healthy relationships in all four spaces.

The spatially specific competencies are described on the following pages. The lists are possibilities only. They are neither comprehensive nor exhaustive. As you help others with their lives, you will likely add to the lists.

Public Spatial Competencies

Public belonging occurs when people connect through an outside influence. People who have a healthy sense of public belonging possess the following competencies:

+ They are able to share a common experience, team, and /or personality without being compelled to pull these relationships "closer."
+ They practice social conformity. They abide by socially accepted rules and practices for public life.
+ They develop the skills to welcome strangers as belongers.

+ They participate significantly in one-time, episodic, and/or site-specific ways.
+ They find appropriate visual focus. This visual focus does not convey a social, personal, or intimate "touch." For example, eye contact for more than a glance communicates a desire to be in a space other than public.

[Who] helped them find their current job. Was it a friend? He kept getting the same reply: No, it was not a friend. It was just an acquaintance. This reminded Granovetter of the classic chemistry lesson demonstrating how weak hydrogen bonds hold huge water molecules together, and that image, stuck in his mind since his freshman year, inspired his first research paper, a long, revealing manuscript on the importance of the weak social ties in our lives. ...

In *The Strength of Weak Ties* Granovetter proposed something that sounds preposterous at first: When it comes to finding a job, getting news, launching a restaurant, or spreading the latest fad, our weak social ties are more important than our cherished strong friendships.[2]

Albert-László Barabási, *Linked: The New Science of Networks*

+ They develop a sense of humor. This humor offers a degree of detachment.
+ They have developed a presence that conveys that they are comfortable in public space and that they mean no harm to those around them.
+ They are comfortable with little or no physical contact.

Social Spatial Competencies

Social belonging occurs when we share "snapshots" of who we are. People who have a healthy sense of social belonging have the following competencies:

+ They can formulate a congruent, authentic snapshot of who they are and what it may be like to have a relationship with them in personal space. This "self" matches both who they are and who they are becoming with the surrounding social setting.
+ They can discern when others are projecting a congruent, authentic "self."

65

+ They have developed the ability to help others create their own their snapshots by creating a social environment that both permits and promotes healthy self-projection.

+ They are comfortable with spontaneous, and sometimes short, interaction.

+ They have harmony between defensive and offensive practices.

+ They are tactful.

+ They have the ability to play and/or organize purposely engineered social games.

+ They are able to keep pleasant visual contact with others in social space. Eye contact comes through short glances—long enough not to be rude, but brief enough not to stare.

+ They can maintain a "working consensus" with those sharing the social space.

+ They are comfortable with physical contact that has little or no meaning.

"The Party"

At a party with ten guests, none of whom initially knows one another, social ties form as the guests start chatting in small groups. At first, the groups are isolated from each other. Indeed, though there are social links between those in the same group, everyone outside of that group is still a stranger. As time goes on, three guests move to different groups and a giant cluster emerges. Although not everyone knows everyone else, there is now a single social network that includes all the guests. By following the social links, one can now find a path between any two guests.[3]

Albert-László Barabási, *Linked: The New Science of Networks*

+ They have developed a skill for "sorting" others into appropriate spaces and can move relationships to those spaces with a natural ease.

+ They have developed the social graces of a neighbor.

Personal Spatial Competencies

Personal belonging occurs when we share private (but not "naked") experiences, feelings, and thoughts. People who have a healthy sense of personal belonging have the following competencies:

+ They keep confidences.

+ They maintain eye contact for extended periods of time without it being an uncomfortable experience for themselves or for those in personal space with them. The relatively short distance provides a clear and focused view of the face.

+ They share private information without sharing too much. Sharing too much would create an uncomfortable experience for themselves or those in personal space with them.

+ They have developed the ability to nurture an interest in another person's private information.

+ They possess the skills to begin, grow, and maintain a one-on-one relationship.

+ They are comfortable with meaningful physical contact—contact that has no intimate sexual context.

Intimate Spatial Competencies

Intimate belonging occurs when we share "naked" information and are not ashamed. People who have a healthy sense of intimate belonging have the following competencies:

+ They have developed an ability to share *who they are* over and against *what they do*. They share definitions of the "naked" self rather than defining themselves by their roles.

+ They have a solid self-definition—they know who their "authentic" self is. This definition is the accumulation of their core self (mentally, spiritually, emotionally, and physically) and their traits, gifts, needs, and desires.

+ They do not share their naked selves indiscriminately.

+ *Community Happens Spontaneously*

In all four spaces, community emerges. And in all four spaces, people hope to connect spontaneously. Anything else feels contrived and out of place. Natasha relates the following:

> I started attending the local library book club. I was really interested in the opening book they were going to review that season. I was planning on only attending the few weeks that this particular book was to be discussed.
>
> The first week, I met Molly. She and I really hit it off. She was only there for the first book and her exit plan sounded strangely familiar.
>
> We are now in our third season attending the book club. I am not interested in most of the books we review. I go to sit with Molly. We have never been to each other's homes. We don't see each other outside of the club meetings. We really don't even talk very much at the meetings. It's just good to know she is going to be there to sit next to.

So often our small group models encourage *forced belonging*. We surmise that putting people into groups will alleviate the emptiness so prevalent in our fast-paced culture.

We think that if the groups we create have a common set of values, meet regularly, and share a covenant, participants will experience belonging. Sometimes this works. Sometimes it almost works. More times than not, it does not work, and, in extremes, it can wound and scar, as in the following story:

> They came home from Promise Keepers on a spiritual high. Six or seven of them, including the pastor, formed a small group. After a couple of months, the relationships began to gel.
>
> During one particularly intense session, two of the men confessed sexual fantasies about women who weren't their wives. There were prayers with arms around each other, and even some tears. Caught up in the emotion of the moment, the pastor admitted that he, too, had entertained inappropriate thoughts toward a woman in the church. The climate changed. The group prayed for him, too, but with more fear than fervor.
>
> The confession given with the expectation of privacy was instead leaked to the congregational grapevine. Within six months, the pastor was gone. Soon thereafter, his wife left him.
>
> Oh, by the way, the small group dissolved, too.

It doesn't take a situation this dramatic to kill a small group. The very agenda of a typical small group gathering may be its demise. Participants become confused as to what space they are to belong in. We cause this by the mixed messages we send that promote inappropriate spatial belonging.

As people arrive there is a buzz of casual, social connection. Finger foods and soft drinks ease the group into a mixing mood. After the allotted time, we move into a more structured formation—sitting in a circle. This spatial conversion tells everyone, "Now we're going to get more personal." What happens next—a litany of prayer requests, only one person talking at a time, someone surfacing as the leader, and longer periods of eye contact—confirm this transformation.

The level of information becomes personal. Those in the room move mentally into a personal space. Some experience belonging. Others wish for another round of finger food.

Sometimes we encourage the group to become even more "intimate." We try to get everyone to grow "closer." However, there are usually too many people gathered for the group to become intimate. On the rare occasion when this happens, some—if not most—describe the experience as "going too far" as they travel home in their cars.

Such experiences are confusing and create an unidentified discomfort. Here are some suggestions as to why this happens.

+ Most join the group hoping for a significant *social* connection. They are looking for neighbors. More on this in chapter 6, but for now let us say that our culture yearns for significant social connections. People are searching for those who will care for them, but at an appropriate distance. They seek those who can help them discover who they are. They would not consider it "bad" to remain in social space for the duration of the group. Small group pastors have described these groups as ones that are "not working," when in fact these groups may be among the healthiest groups the pastor has.

+ Some come to a small group seeking a *personal* connection. The problem is the group may be too large for a healthy connection to form. The likelihood that eight to twelve people in the same room all have the need—and the competencies—to find personal space with one another are slim. This is especially true if they have been forced together by random selection. There is a greater likelihood of personal belonging emerging spontaneously in a group that self-organizes. Plus, most people who seek friends in personal space are looking for only one or two personal friends—not eight or a dozen.

+ We also muddle things by building expectations of *intimacy*. In fact, this is what we hope, promote, and plan for. It would be far healthier to promote social or personal connection, leaving intimacy to groups with an appropriate number of people. Two is a good number.

It may be that when people are forced together there are just enough healthy people who find some connection that community actually materializes. Our orchestration of who is in the group may not have anything to do with whether the group gels. Antonio relates the following:

> I have a time when all newcomers gather at my house to find out more about the congregation and to connect with other newcomers. At the end of the evening, I used to ask the new-comers to choose a small group from a list of existing groups I supplied to them. Very few ever found their own way to a group. It was only through a "healthy" amount of prodding that some would try this daunting request.
>
> One night someone had the courage to ask, "Why can't *we* just gather as a new group?" Several controlling thoughts rushed through my head. Who would lead? How can a bunch of new-comers know what to do?
>
> I nervously allowed them to meet. It is now the only way I approach small groups. Sometimes people find a connection that night, other times they do not and I have learned to be at peace about it. I no longer try to control their lives. A new group begins when people connect naturally.

People long to belong, and so are in constant search for connection. As leaders, we can no longer take advantage of this. We cannot permit ourselves to label "authentic" only those connections *we* create for *them*. We can no longer pretend that forced community works better than, or as well as, what really works—the community that arises when human beings spontaneously connect.

But is there no way we can help? Should we stop creating

groups? Can we plan spontaneity? Nothing really happens without leadership—does it?

Most leaders genuinely try to help people. However, in our zeal we are tempted to pay more attention to fads than to what really helps. Books on small groups, tapes, seminars, and models abound, yet few of us achieve more than a 30 to 35 percent participation rate.

Greg is the small group pastor of a megachurch. He is considered highly successful. He was gracious enough to grant me an interview, of which the following is a portion:

Joe: So, Greg, what makes a successful small group in your system?

Greg: Well, we measure success in several ways. First, we want to know if people are connecting. Are people becoming close to the group and God.

Second, we want to measure how many people are attending every week. We want to know how many in the congregation are involved in a small group.

We believe that this is the most significant place where people grow their relationship with God. We really don't want anyone to attend here without experiencing a small group.

Joe: This seems to be a vital part of your ministry philosophy.

Greg: Yes it is. It is a part of the DNA of our church. Everything we do builds off the small group relationship.

Joe: So you must have a high percentage of people attending small groups. What percentage attends each week and how many do you currently have?

Greg: It is sort of hard to say. We believe that we have about 30 to 35 percent involved in a weekly small group experience. And, we have somewhere between 200 and 225 [small groups].

Thirty to thirty-five percent! Is that success? Even more troubling to me is the "[e]verything we do builds off the small group relationship" philosophy. What kind of pressure are we putting on the congregation and ourselves if we expect—or worse, require—everyone to have a small group experience?

I am convinced that most small group pastors realize that 100 percent participation is a fantasy. I also believe that most small group pastors are aware that only a fraction of the 30 to 35 percent who do participate are actually being helped.

But we are so afraid of failure that we tack supports on this leaning tower to make it look like it is standing on its own. We want to believe our programs work. And we want to keep our jobs! Admitting failure is not an option.

How can we keep our dignity and let go at the same time?

If we break this cycle, will it just lead us to another fruitless one?

+ *The Secret of Slime Mold (Emergence Theory)*

The slime mold spends much of its life as thousands of distinct single-celled units, each moving separately from its other comrades. Under the right conditions, those myriad cells will coalesce again into a single, larger organism, which then begins its leisurely crawl across the garden floor, consuming rotting leaves and wood as it moves about. When the environment is less hospitable, the slime mold acts as a single organism; when the weather turns cooler and the mold enjoys a large food supply, "it" becomes a "they." The slime mold oscillates between being a single creature and a swarm.[4]

The intriguing secret of slime mold is that there is no "master planner" calling the cells to unite. The coming together is spontaneous. There is no apparent leader. There is no call to action. No vision statements, value statements, or mission statements. There is no "queen bee" or charismatic leader. The cells collect spontaneously when the environment triggers the response.

When slime mold encounters a favorable environment, the mold emits a substance called acrasin or cyclic AMP. When this occurs, the slime mold cells unite with others in the area.

When people encounter someone to whom they are attracted, there is a similar occurrence. The triggering mechanism? For people, there are several. Human beings communicate their desire to connect through eye dilation, facial expression (sometimes voluntary, sometimes involuntary), posture, body temperature, and, yes, we too emit chemicals called pheremones, which are decoded by those around us.

When there is a favorable environment we make spontaneous choices regarding to whom we want to belong. This is the type of connection that people are looking for in their lives.

Slime mold offers us an interesting insight: We humans could help by creating the healthy environments in which people naturally connect. If we would concentrate upon facilitating the environment instead of the result (people experiencing community), we might see healthy, spontaneous community emerge.

> Monastics have relearned what Saint Benedict knew, and have in turn taught me, that real community is a gift, not something you construct. There is nearly everywhere today an intense, even desperate, longing to experience "I am because you are," and people are devising all sorts of schemes for "building community." The monastery is a living witness to the truth that community is something that happens when the environment is right, when hospitality is grounded in discipline and discernment, when prayer and work are rightly ordered. The Rule does not construct community. It hints at the necessary conditions.[5]
>
> **Patrick Henry, *The Ironic Christian's Companion: Finding the Marks of God's Grace in the World***

+ *Group Environmentalist or Group Programmer?*

"Environmentalists" practice restraint when it comes to controlling the results. They are primarily concerned with creating a "healthy" climate for spontaneity to occur. They develop simple environmental parameters and then sit back to see what happens. "Programmers," on the other hand, take control.

If we are to allow people full opportunities to belong, we must switch from being group programmers to becoming group environmentalists. It starts with giving up control.

Too often we press our good intentions to excess. We don't help people; we control people. We enjoy the power of knowing the best road to someone else's well-being. Isn't it fun pointing them down the right road and leading them along the way?

We assume that *we* grow and lead people. The truth is that often we are merely growing and leading ourselves. As Kennon Callahan so aptly states, "only you can grow you."[6] In the same way, only *you* can lead *you*.

Yes, we can be of *some* help to others as they grow and lead their own lives forward. But we do not grow and lead people; only they can do that. We like to believe that we hold the answers people need in order to grow, because if we hold those truths, we hold the power and control.

It is time to give up the intoxicating need to control other people's lives. It is time to start leading our own lives in healthy ways. People need us to help in healthy ways, not controlling ways. This is the "holy grail" for which people are searching in the promise of belonging. They want help in healthy ways, they want to connect in healthy ways, and they want to experience family in healthy ways.

[
If we really knew the God of Jesus, we would stop trying to control and manipulate others "for their own good," knowing full well that this is not how God works among his people.[7]

Brennan Manning, The Signature of Jesus
]

We must also refocus our energy toward "chemistry." An environmentalist massages the "chemical compounds" that produce the environment. He tries to cultivate fertile soil in which spontaneous phenomena can occur. Gardeners know this well. Azaleas, for example, require very acidic soil; roses prefer soil with moderate acidity. Both plants will survive and even grow a little in the same landscape bed, but it is unlikely that both will thrive simultaneously in that same bed.

+ Cultivating Fertile Soil

Chemical compounds have specific, unique identifiers. H_2O is water only if there are two parts hydrogen and one part oxygen. The equation cannot be altered and still represent water.

The "community compound" may also have an equation. I suggest it looks something like $Pu_8S_4P_2I$. For every one part significant intimate belonging, there are two parts personal, four parts social, and eight parts public.

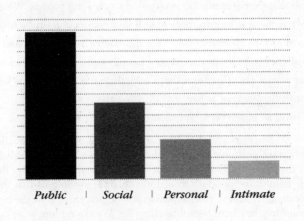

Public | Social | Personal | Intimate

When the community compound is altered, healthy belonging may not exist.

Many promote this as the compound for community: $C_{SV}C_{VF}FMCC$ (a common set of values plus a common vision of the future plus frequent meetings plus a formal or informal contractual covenant). These are not the ingredients *for* community, but rather the results *of* community.

We can cultivate fertile soil for spontaneous community if we focus on helping people build the competencies they need to grow healthy connections in each of the four spaces. Our research might be less concerned with new "icebreaker games" and focused instead on what helps people connect in social space. We might spend less time reading "how-to" books on small groups and more time discovering new ways to connect people through outside influences (public space). We might quit pushing children to express all their emotions in public and teach them instead the appropriate spaces in which to share intimate thoughts and the cries of hurt and anger.

The $Pu_8S_4P_2I$ chemical compound will alter our approach to groups as well. It is not healthy to promote only small groups as the most valid way to find community. Doing so is far too limiting. We must instead promote a healthy ratio of different kinds of groups. Group environmentalists pay attention to the chemical compound for community and regard connections in all for spaces as significant.

We shape environments, as opposed to creating groups. When the environment is healthy, people will find connection on their own and form groups spontaneously. This approach gives freedom and responsibility to individuals, because people will experience belonging and a sense that this helps them with their life. It also helps keep our controlling nature at bay.

Claire, a church secretary, tells us,

> When they call the office and ask to be placed in a small group we politely encourage them to begin to gather with a few of their friends. This is the type of small group we are now finding helpful for people's lives. Individuals are telling us that this spontaneity and self-organization has helped them find the relationships they have been searching for. We are no longer in control—and that's a great feeling.

Talk with any coach who has successfully created a team and he or she will tell you that yes, he or she tried their best to develop a team spirit, but all of a sudden it just arose out of nowhere—it developed spontaneously. The team had "chemistry."

Listen to healthy persons talk about their lives and you will hear about connections they have with people who don't know their names, conversations they have with acquaintances, the fun they have with close friends, and the deep affection they have for a select few. Relationships in all four spaces. Further, the conversation will allude to all of these connections being spontaneous, not forced; "environmental" and not controlled; "chemical" and not planned.

Kevin Kelly, a leading thinker in the properties of emergent theory, traced several characteristics of emergence back to William

Morton Wheeler's research on the behavior of ants. As Howard Rheingold points out in *Smart Mobs*, "Kelly drew parallels between the ways both biological and artificial 'vivi-systems' exhibit the same four characteristics of what he called 'swarm systems':

+ the absence of imposed centralized control
+ the autonomous nature of subunits
+ the high connectivity between the subunits
+ the webby nonlinear causality of peers influencing peers"[8]

Rheingold continues:

Individual fish and birds (and tight-formation fighter pilots) school and flock simply by paying attention to what their nearest neighbors do. The coordinated movements of schools and flocks is a dynamically shifting aggregation of individual decisions. Even if there were a central tuna or pigeon who could issue orders, no system of propagating orders from a central source can operate swiftly enough to avoid being eaten by sharks or slamming into trees. When it comes to hives and swarms, the emergent capabilities of decentralized self-organization can be surprisingly intelligent.

What happens when the individuals in a tightly coordinated group are more highly intelligent creatures rather than simpler organisms like insects or birds? How do humans exhibit emergent behavior? As soon as this question occurred to me, I immediately recall the story Kevin Kelly told at the beginning of *Out of Control*, his 1994 book about the emergent behaviors in biology, machinery, and human affairs. He described an event at an annual film show for computer graphics professionals. A small paddle was attached to each seat in the auditorium, with reflective material of contrasting colors on each side of the paddle. The screen in the auditorium displayed a high-contrast, real-time video view of the audience. The person leading the exercise, computer graphics wizard Loren Carpenter, asked those on one side of the auditorium aisle to hold the paddles with one color showing and asked the other half of the audience to hold up the opposite color. Then, following Carpenter's suggestions, the audience self-organized a dot that moved around the screen, added a couple of paddles on the screen, and began to play a giant game of self-organized video Pong, finally creating a graphical representation of an airplane and flying it around the screen. Like flocks, there was no central control of the exercise after Carpenter made a suggestion. Members of the audience paid attention to what their neighbors were doing and what was happening on the screen.[9]

Notice that "spontaneous" does not mean "random." Emergent theory proposes that with a few environmental "suggestions," sudden epidemics of cooperation arise. But it takes the suggestions to create the soil in which the chaotic order can emerge. Much like Carpenter's suggestions to the audience, these slight controls provide the "heralding voice" for spontaneous group decisions.

In 1998, Duncan Watts and Steve Strogatz came upon a graph that plotted the social puzzle dubbed "Six Degrees of Separation," which asserts that every person on the planet can be seemingly connected to any other person within six steps. They tried a number of ordered graph calculations and random theories of graphing, yet none seemed to answer this small-world conundrum. "Then finally, on that winter's day in 1998, the two researchers stumbled over their peculiar graph. What they discovered was a subtle way of connecting the dots that was neither orderly nor random but somewhere in-between, an unusual pattern with chaos mingling in equal balance with order."[10]

Leonard Sweet, who enjoys the art of creating new terms from two existing words, has used the term "chaordic" to describe this phenomenon. ("Chaordic" was coined by Dee Hock, the president of VISA, to describe how his company works.)

Community emerges when there is a "chaordic harmony" of belonging. Trying to organize this is much like trying to organize a boat bobbing in the ocean. People connect spontaneously but not randomly. This is good news. It means we have the ability to help. If social connections were random, we would have little hope of bringing help.

+ *What About Karen?*

Karen, the friendly waitress introduced in chapter 3, teaches us many things. First, her words tell us that she has connections in at least three of the four spaces. "On the street" refers to public space. "Parties or hang out in clubs" alludes to her search for social connection. And when she refers to a "really close" friend, she is speaking of her personal space.

It seems that Karen has never learned that these connections are significant—in the space that they exist now. She may have an innate feeling that to be significant, relationships must be personal or intimate. She is trying to make every connection significant by attempting to pull every connection "close," diligently trying to move relationships into a space in which people neither want nor need to belong. She is trying to grow all her relationships in the same soil.

Help for Karen may exist in the "chemistry" of community. It may be as simple as helping her to recognize that the connections she has are significant. We could teach her how to grow these connections in harmony with the "chemical compound." We could help her grow her understanding of how to recognize significance in all four spaces.

The answer is not to control Karen's growth. It may be more helpful to invite her into healthy environments and allow her to witness significant connections as these connections emerge in all four spaces.

+ Measuring Spontaneity, Community, and Belonging

What organizations measure becomes important. Likewise, individuals measure what they find important in their lives. Measuring is not bad. However, many times we measure the wrong things, things that then take on an importance they do not deserve. I find that we measure what is easiest to quantify. If something is difficult to quantify, we try to find something similar that is not quite so difficult to count, and we measure that.

Spontaneity is difficult to measure, so many organizations do not measure it. And since they cannot measure it, it loses its importance. Yet people "count" the spontaneity in their lives all the time. They do not measure numerically, saying "I've had five spontaneous experiences today." Instead, they tell the story of the encounter:

+ "I met someone very interesting in the deli today."
+ "I had a great time at the concert. The crowd was really into it. We had such a good time."
+ "It was as if we had known each other all our lives."

Stories are the measuring tools of spontaneity, of community, and of belonging. Organizationally, we can measure the spontaneous experiences of community by listening for the stories people share. Then it is our responsibility to tell and retell the stories to create an organizational climate of belonging.

[
Deadlines, schedules, meetings, the workday itself—all move to the ticking of time's moments. The Web, on the other hand, reminds us that the fundamental unit of time isn't a moment, it's a story, and the string that holds time together isn't the mere proximity of moments but our interest in the story.[11]

David Weinberger, *Small Pieces Loosely Joined: A Unified Theory of the Web*
]

Belonging cannot be measured in numbers. You may count attendance, but to give a conclusive number for those in your congregation who experience community is impossible. The stories we collect, however, help put together the community puzzle. Says Etienne Wenger, "Stories are a powerful component of any culture, and legitimizing the storytelling process encourages people to act out the stories they would like one day to tell."[12]

Using stories as the measuring rod brings a dynamic energy to your community. Stories connect in ways that numbers cannot. Yet because of their complex, chaordic message, stories can also raise troubling questions.

If we change the measuring tool, it may lead us to conclude that we need to question our definition of congregation. Who belongs to this congregation if we measure by story? What about those who connect with us without our knowledge?

I have an idea. What if the congregation God has given you is all of those who experience a connection? Granting that this may be true, and realizing that we have no idea how many actually connect, what if we were to assume they are a part of us and give them an opportunity to "opt out" rather than to "opt in"? To put it another way, what if we were to assume that everyone who is in some way connected to our congregation belongs until they specifically indicate that they do not?

"We do that already," you may say. "If they do not come to our weekend worship or participate in some way, they have opted out." Yet, as we have seen, people can connect in ways other than coming to "our place." What would change if we treated everyone as if they belonged?

[
A story doesn't thread events together like beads on a string; it instead keeps us in thrall by promising us an ending that was there, hiding, in the beginning all along. Our time is bound together by the stories we hear, tell, and tell to ourselves. A story is an expression of how the world matters to us and thus interest, passion, caring—fire—thread our time.[13]

David Weinberger, _Small Pieces_
Loosely Joined: A Unified Theory of the Web
]

As stated in the introduction, as words such as *family, neighbor,* and *friend* are redefined, we may need to find a new definition for those who encompass "congregation."

+ *Environments Are Changed One Person at a Time*

The middle school principal was forced to make a tough decision. The school year was about to start, and enrollments in fourth grade were significantly lower than they had been the previous year. She would have to move a fourth-grade teacher to fifth grade. But whom should she move?

It had been tense last year, particularly among the fifth-grade teachers. Relationships in that group would probably be strained this year, too. The principal announced her decision: "Marilyn is moving from fourth grade to fifth grade. She's going to be team-teaching with Beth."

This was good news to the fourth-grade teachers; they didn't like Marilyn. They thought she was a good teacher, but way too much of a nitpicker. She kept records of everything.

This was not good news to Beth. She had had some difficult years with the other fifth-grade teachers. Now she was supposed to share her classroom with Marilyn?

That August, Marilyn and Beth began their team teaching. Many days did not go well. Marilyn's nitpicking put Beth in a bad mood. Beth's bad moods were scrupulously recorded in Marilyn's journal. This tension in grade five began to spill over into the rest of the school.

In March, all of the teachers attended the required staff meeting. In this, as in all monthly staff meetings, the principal offered an opportunity for any individual to express gratitude toward another teacher or staff member.

This time, Marilyn spoke up. Nervously she began, "I would like to tell all of you how much I appreciate Beth." Marilyn continued, mentioning Beth's kindness, excellence as a teacher, and her support. Everyone sat up straighter, listening in amazement. By the time Marilyn had finished, the climate had changed. New attitudes emerged. A new environment, one of community admiration, started to develop. For the first time that school year, the fifth-grade teachers began to come together.

The day after the meeting, Beth sent this e-mail to the entire staff:

I wanted very much yesterday morning to respond to what Marilyn shared in the staff meeting, but there are times when feelings cannot be expressed through words. Yesterday was one of those occasions. Even if the words had come, they couldn't possibly have squeezed past the lump in my throat.

Marilyn is a person of integrity, determination, wisdom, dignity, intelligence, compassion, humor and, as we witnessed yesterday, a person of great courage. She is a treasure, and I count it an honor to work with her.

How appropriate that part of our meeting focused on esteem building. Marilyn gave the perfect lesson on how to do just that. I'm sure everyone present recognized the fact that she was speaking straight from her heart. Those heartfelt words boosted my esteem more than anything else could. No other award or honor I have ever received meant more to me than her words yesterday. I will cherish that moment forever. Thank you, Marilyn, for that gift. Many of you share with me her compliment. I have some trusted colleagues in my grade level and many dear friends throughout the school who care about, support, and challenge me. You give me the strength and courage to say and do the things that I think need to be said and done. Thank you for helping me to be a better person.

I want to say a couple more things before closing. This school was once a great school, not a perfect school, but a great one. We can make it that way again if we choose to. Let's get back to one of the things we do really well—care for each other. This is a very caring staff. We do so many acts of kindness for our students, but sometimes we don't do enough for ourselves or each other. Maybe we can work on getting to know each other better. As Marilyn said yesterday, she and I have been here many years, but never really knew each other until this year. There are many people here with big hurts. Maybe all they need is a smile or five minutes of a listening ear. You never can be sure what others are going through or what your act of kindness may mean to them.

As I write this, I'm thinking to myself. . . Am I willing to do this? Do I have enough care and concern inside me to give to others? What about those with whom I have a conflict? I don't have all of the answers, but I do know that I want to be more caring tomorrow than I am today.

One last thing. I truly hope that at some point in your career you have the opportunity to feel as special as I did yesterday. Thank you.

Sincerely,

Beth

Change did not begin with the group, but with an individual. Neither could the change have taken place if it had been forced. The principal could not have required it. She could not have affected it with a lecture on teamwork. Belonging does not grow from rules, order, or education. Community emerges from the environment.

One change in the environment can change the harmony and health of the community. One person can create an environment for health and healing.

It is worth saying again: People search for spontaneous community, not forced belonging. Permit people to lead themselves. God does. We can learn from him.

When we provide a nurturing environment, people will find their own ways to healthy connection.

[
When you select the "update" link on your mobile's ImaHima menu, everyone on your buddy list knows, for example, that you are within a few blocks of Shibuya station and are free for lunch.
The just-in-time, just-in-place matchmaking services for strangers, an intriguing aspect of ImaHima, is also where the most caution is required.[14]

Howard Rheingold, *Smart Mobs: The Next Social Revolution*
]

+ [*consider*]

+ How uncomfortable are you with spontaneity? Do you always need to be in control?

+ What stories from your life and the life of the congregation exhibit healthy community?

+ What storytelling outlets do you have in place? Are there other opportunities that would make sense to develop as storytelling environments?

+ When considering the community chemical compound, list the significant belongings in your life and in your congregation's life. Are there any discoveries?

+ Have you ever had the experience of seeing a group self organize in a spontaneous manner? What was the situation? Did the group exhibit health? Was it fun?

[*five*]

trading spaces

Life may not be much of a gamble, but interaction is.[1]

**Erving Goffman, "The Presentation of
Self in Everyday Life: Selections"**

I was at a small group conference to research material for this book. Some of the best material came from an unexpected source.

A friend introduced me to Sue, who was part of the behind-the-scenes team for the meeting. Sue and I started talking about the four spaces, and I explained my ideas on how the four spaces could provide a template for healthy belonging. After about half an hour of discussion, Sue asked, "How do you see this helping the average person—you know, someone like me?"

I responded by sharing the story of Tom and his mother, Ramona. Tom was not a "Mama's boy," but as he was growing up, he and his mother had a close, solid relationship. When Tom came home from school, Ramona never had to pry the day's activities out of him. She knew his friends and his dreams.

Tom continued to share details of his life with his mother as he grew older, even talking about dating and girlfriends. They were mother and son. They were also intimate friends.

Tom fell in love with Janelle. They dated through college, and got married soon after graduation. The wedding was everything a wedding is supposed to be. Both sets of in-laws had grown friendly, and all were confident about the couple's future.

The two had been married for about a year when they moved several states away so Tom could accept a position in a prestigious law firm. It didn't take Ramona long to recognize that Tom had not only moved geographically, but he had also moved to a different space in the family.

Ramona was not prepared for this. She knew that her relationship with her son would change somewhat with Tom's marriage, but she expected him to belong to the family as he always had—intimately. She did not anticipate that the saying, "Marry a daughter, gain a son; marry a son, lose a son" would be true in her life.

Tom's parents visited several times over the next three years, even spending a week with the young couple in a lakefront cabin. Ramona and Tom spoke about once a week by phone.

Tom's work brought him back to his hometown. Ramona said to herself, "Now it will be the way it was before." But it was not. Tom and Janelle now had an eighteen-month-old. Plus they were active in their church. Tom never seemed to have the time he once had for his mother.

Ramona limited her phone calls to once a week. Strangely, the calls—across town now, no longer long distance—contained much the same content as before. Yet an innocent question such as "Can we get together soon?" seemed intrusive, both to Ramona as she asked it and to Tom as he heard it.

Both Tom and Ramona knew that what Ramona was really asking was, "Why are we so distant? Don't you want to be part of the family any more?" Her own son seemed like a stranger to her.

The situation was difficult for Tom as well. He felt pressured between the needs of his wife and child and the needs of his mother.

Tom had "traded spaces." He had to. After getting married, how could he possibly continue to belong in the same intimate space with his mother? Tom's wife and child now occupied his intimate space. He still wanted to belong to the family of his childhood, but he could not belong in the same way.

(I could see that the story I was telling touched some familiar experience in Sue. Her eyes brimmed. Her face expressed a mixture of regret and hope.)

Ramona and I talked. She was confused and hurt. She didn't understand why Tom did not want to "be part of the family anymore." She felt as if she had been replaced. I shared with Ramona my thoughts of belonging in four spaces and how people can handle only a limited amount of intimate connection. I told her that it wasn't that Tom didn't want to be a part of the family. In fact, he needed to belong more than ever—but in a different space. He needed significant belonging to the family in a social space.

As I finished telling this story, Sue did not cry. But it was several minutes before she spoke. "You don't know how much you have just helped me," she said.

A few weeks later she sent me this e-mail:

Joseph,

Thanks for your willingness to share your thinking and passion with me. Its instant application with my foster daughter, Sarah, was almost haunting. I want to share with you the outcome. I'm on my way home from Sarah's college graduation. It was probably the richest time I've ever had with her. In part because I let go of trying to persuade her to have the "intimate" relationship with her biological parents and the larger more rewarding part was allowing her to claim that space with me. The calm, the peace, and the delight of our time together cannot be put into words. But even my husband noticed a dramatic change (and is still trying to figure it out!).

Thank you for your authentic self and for touching my soul.

Blessings,

Sue

It is important to recognize that *no relationship survives in one space for the entire life of the relationship.* We move among the four spaces throughout the life of *all* relationships. Many times, we do so unconsciously and without effort.

Throughout this book, I have deliberately tried to separate the four spaces for examination purposes only. But in fact they are not as distinct and defined as I have made them appear for purposes of explanation. They are fluid, not concrete.

Consider the situation of Max and Annie. For decades they had looked forward to retirement. He spent forty years on the assembly line in a car factory; she waited until the children were grown and took a job in a neighborhood law office, working her way up to the position of administrative assistant. Over countless meals and Sunday drives, Max and Annie talked about and dreamed about and carefully planned every detail of their future. They achieved their goal, both retiring on the same day.

> If we can rid ourselves of the need for a single explanation, and if we can think of man as surrounded by a series of expanding and contracting fields which provide information of many kinds, we shall begin to see him in an entirely different light. We can then begin to learn about human behavior, including personality types.[2]
>
> **Edward T. Hall, *The Hidden Dimension***

The first few months were a dream come true. First, they visited each of the kids. Next came the long-hoped-for trip to Hawaii and on to Australia. After the trip, it was back to the same old routine. Four decades on the 7 to 3 shift meant that Max needed no alarm clock. Annie was an early riser, too. Morning after morning they got up before dawn, sat at the table drinking coffee, and waited for the day.

Six months into retirement, Max started a new job. Retirement had provided a lot of firsts. First time for a six-week vacation. First time Annie felt crowded by her husband's presence. First time they had more arguments than conversations.

"He drove me crazy!" Annie says. "He was underfoot all the time. Worse than a child. I had my own way of doing things around the house. Now *he* wanted to do everything. He wouldn't leave me alone!"

Max piped in, "After a week or so we couldn't find anything to talk about. We spent every moment together—what *was* there to talk about?"

That was six years ago, and there are no plans to retire again. Max smiles and explains, "We love each other too much to spend every moment together. That was just too close for comfort."

When we step back from the stories of Tom and his mother, Sue and her daughter, and Max and Annie, we can see how the ways in which they belonged changed. The same is true for everyone. Sometimes the changes correspond with the seasons of our lives. Sometimes the changes are expected, sometimes unexpected.

> I came upon her late one evening on a deserted street in Hyde Park, a relatively affluent neighborhood in an otherwise mean, impoverished section of Chicago. As I swung onto the avenue behind her, there seemed to be a discreet, uninflammatory distance between us. Not so. She cast back a worried glance. To her, the youngish black man—a broad six feet two inches with a beard and billowing hair, both hands shoved into the pockets of a bulky military jacket—seemed menacingly close. After a few more quick glimpses, she picked up her pace and was soon running in earnest. Within seconds she disappeared into a cross street.
>
> That was more than a decade ago. I was twenty-two years old, a graduate student newly arrived at the University of Chicago. It was in the echo of that terrified woman's footfalls that I first began to know the unwieldy inheritance I'd come into—the ability to alter public space in ugly ways.[3]

Because our perception of space is in our minds, it changes as someone approaches us, enters the room, or joins a conversation. In a moment's notice, relationships can change.

At the movie theater I paid for the tickets, and my wife, my daughter, and I selected our seats. We like to be as close to the middle as we can, and there were plenty of seats because we were so early. Jaclyn sat in the center, Sara and I on either side of her. We talked, ate popcorn, and tried to answer the trivia questions on the screen. A few minutes before the lights dimmed, I excused myself and went to find the restroom.

When I returned, I noticed that a gentleman had elected to sit in the seat next to my wife. There were plenty of other seats to choose from—especially for a single person. Why did he choose *that* seat? I could see that Sara was uncomfortable; the relaxed conversation that I had left was now quieted.

A few moments later, the man's wife joined him. Her presence changed the mood of our family. Sara's tense posture relaxed, and we all enjoyed the movie. People entering and exiting our space affects our spatial connections. But external and internal experiences can cause us to trade spaces, too.

> Sometimes one partner can't cope and will simply opt out of the marriage or excessively maintain independence within it, leaving the committed spouse grappling for a sense of marital interdependence.[4]
>
> **Pamela Paul, *The Starter Marriage and the Future of Matrimony***

Mary's marriage is typical. It has its rough edges, but for the most part she and Henry have a caring relationship. They raised two daughters and recently welcomed their first grandchild into the family. Life is good.

For over twenty years, Henry has climbed poles for the local cable company. He works hard and directs a crew of thirty, yet his future is uncertain. There is talk at the cable company about cutting back. Henry is at that dangerous age: he's been working long enough to have seniority, but also long enough to be expensive. Two of his contemporaries have already been forced to retire.

Henry has had his share of on-the-job injuries. Two were falls from a pole, resulting in painful surgeries and extended absences from his job. He's worried about how this will affect his employer's layoff decisions. To make matters worse, four members of Henry's extended family developed bipolar disorder and severe depression as they neared his present age. "It must run in the family," he keeps saying to himself.

The job. The injuries. The "family curse." The more Henry thinks about it, the more he withdraws.

Mary does not know what to do. "He doesn't want to talk about it," she explains. "The other day he laid down on the couch while I made supper. When I said it was time to eat, he yelled at me and told me to leave him alone. He was hateful, and that's not his way."

Mary continued, "Two days ago I asked him about something we needed to decide and he yelled at me again: 'Shut up—just shut up! Could you do that?' I know he's worried. But he's taking it all out on me. I don't even know if he still loves me."

All of us experience times when we want to suffer alone. During such times we may move those around us into a different space. Things can change quickly. Some occasion for joy or excitement—perhaps something as simple as the first warm day of spring—can cause us to alter the way we want to belong to someone.

"Demystifying the Adoption Option"

Eleven years ago, I arrived at the funeral of my brother-in-law as both a mourning relative and the sudden legal guardian of his two children. It was the family's second funeral in the course of a year. Nine months earlier, my sister-in-law, niece and nephew had died in a tragic accident. People approached me, pressed my hands and said, "You are so wonderful to take these children."

It was a noble view of adoption, with me the rescuer, the saver of children. It was tempting to buy into it, and I did at times. But once I got down to the business of raising children, I found that that perspective had little to do with the reality of creating a family. . . .

Despite my best efforts at forging a relationship with her, my daughter gave me the cold shoulder for the first five years she was with us. Her favorite story was "Cinderella," and I'm fairly certain I wasn't the Fairy Godmother.

I have a friend who became a full-time stepmother one weekend when her husband's ex-wife decided she could no longer care for the children. She raised the kids, monitoring late-night asthma attacks, baking room-mother treats and sitting through Scout meetings.

"My daughter invited me to the mother's weekend at college," she told me one day. "Then she found out her real mother could make it, so she called back to uninvite me."
I was shocked at her daughter's heartless treatment of the mother who had always been there for her. My friend and I are No. 2—we will never truly be No. 1 in our kids' eyes, and that is one of the not-so-nice realities of adoption.

continued on next page

We are quick to point out what we consider our children's misdirected loyalties, but what of our own? My friend's preference would have been to have raised a traditional family with her husband. Mine was also to have children of my own, which I attempted to do without success for seven years. However much we pretend otherwise, our adopted children were second choices for us.

So there it is. Our children want what they have lost, and so do we. They have lost their blood ties to parents. We have lost our visions of family, the dream of how our lives should look. . . .

A few months ago my 12-year-old daughter called from her grandmother's house, where she was visiting for the week. She has a special bond with this grandmother, the mother of the mother she lost. "I miss the dog," she said, then laughed. "Oh, and I miss you, too." When I hung up, I was glad for all those years that we moved slowly together, circling each other— afraid to place our vulnerability in each other's hands. She did miss me. I could hear it in her voice.

My son is now old enough to understand chromosomes and the steps beyond the mechanics of reproduction. My husband's blood runs through my son, but mine does not, and he knows it. "There is a ceremony," I told him, thinking this would appeal greatly to an 11-year-old boy, "where we can become blood brothers. We can do it if you want." He considered it and said no, I imagine because of the part involving blood. Now I wonder if it was I who wanted the ceremony, if I was still longing for the solidity of a blood bond.

I feel ridiculous for having suggested this idea, realizing he has no need for such things—that he is, in fact, exactly where he should be. He knows where his family is, both the one that is buried and the one that sits at the hockey rink, watching him play. And because he is such a great kid, he is willing to be patient with a mother who sometimes likes to make her mission much more complicated than what it really is: the offering of family, simple, sweet and pure.[5]

Nancy Hanner, *Newsweek*

+ *Everyone Moves*

I was leading a workshop discussing community in our emerging culture when a member of the audience asked, "Is it true that every relationship moves?"

"Yes," I told him.

He was not ready to accept that. "What about my relationship with my family? Can I belong to my wife in public space and stay married? What about my church? I've always assumed that everyone should belong to the church intimately."

He was full of questions: "And what about my relationship with God? I've always preached that the relationship God demands is intimate. I've always invited someone to accept Christ as their *personal* savior. I'm confused!"

Part of this man's confusion comes from the ways we define relationships. These definitions help us categorize the ways we belong and to whom we belong. For example, we describe a relationship between husband and wife as *intimate*. In fact, we may say that this is what defines marriage and that marriage is the most intimate relationship a person should have (except perhaps our connection with God).

These characterizations are useful categories, but they can have damaging effects. Using the example of marriage, let's examine how this can happen. If we enter into marriage thinking the relationship will succeed if it is intimate only, we will soon become disillusioned. No human being can long maintain a level of consistent intimate belonging. This disillusionment will likely pose a threat to the future of the whole relationship.

Take the situation of Pam and Gary. When she called for an appointment, I could tell she was upset. One year ago I had performed their wedding. What was wrong? When I suggested Thursday, she insisted on Monday. "This can't wait," she told me.

I drove into the church parking lot a few minutes early, but they were even earlier. As I led the way toward the building, they followed behind. Gary looked defeated, and it was clear Pam had been crying.

After a few moments, Pam blurted, "He doesn't love me anymore!" She slapped him on the shoulder. "Go ahead—tell him!" She buried her head in her hands, sobbing. Gary looked at me, confused and questioning.

"Pam, that's just not—"

"It *is* true! It *is* true! You aren't interested in me. You'd rather be with everyone else. You don't talk to me. You talk to everyone else. I thought we were supposed to be married. The only time you want to be close is when you want to have sex."

[
During times of conflict, girls will turn on one another with a language and justice only they can understand. Behind a façade of female intimacy lies a terrain traveled in secret, marked with anguish, and nourished by silence.[6]

**Rachel Simmons, *Odd Girl Out:
The Hidden Culture of Aggression in Girls***
]

As I listened, I scrolled down my mental screen looking for helpful wisdom. I tried to remember counseling and psychology courses from my college days. I had trained for such a time, yet the "answers" that sounded so good in classroom role-play were empty now.

My training suggested that I needed to "work" with Gary. It seemed he did not have the ability to express himself intimately beyond sex. Maybe I should discover whether he was encouraged to cry as a boy. Maybe his father had given him too macho a perception of true manhood.

Yet it didn't seem to me that the problem was solely Gary's. Over the next few weeks we discovered what marriage meant to both Gary and Pam. They wrote down and expressed to each other their expectations. We talked over which ones were realistic and which were unrealistic.

Early in the process, both Pam and Gary realized that Pam had entered their marriage expecting a storybook world. She had read too many novels, watched too many movies, and had come to believe that she and Gary would live constantly in intimate harmony.

Pam had never been taught that all relationships—even a marriage—move among all four spaces.

+ *One Relationship, Four Spaces*

Couples teach me that a healthy marriage involves building significant belonging in all four spaces. It is not true that marriage is an intimate relationship only. A solid marriage builds its most significant connections in all four relational spaces between husband and wife.

> The nature of marriage has changed so much. It has become a kind of close friendship with a sexual relationship between a man and a woman. That's a change. Before, it was a multifaceted institution. A partnership that was legally bound, typically a religious partnership, and a partnership between two families. Just because the husband and wife didn't get along wasn't a reason to break up. Also, in times past, men, by and large, had mostly male friends and women had mostly female friends. Today, we're together in an entirely different way. It's stripped down, mainly to the two of them. They're best friends, often isolated, alone, and this is something pretty new.[7]
>
> **Pamela Paul, *The Starter Marriage and the Future of Matrimony***

Spouses Belonging Publicly

Public belonging happens when we connect because of an outside influence. What does it look like for a husband and wife to belong publicly to each other?

The marriage of James Carville and Mary Matalin provides a good example. Carville is a Democrat who served directly under President Bill Clinton. Matalin is a Republican who served directly under Presidents Reagan and George H. W. Bush. Carville and Matalin are both outspoken advocates for their respective parties. Both serve their parties at the highest levels. How do they keep their marriage together?

I have observed them as individuals (in radio or television interviews) and as a couple (in joint public appearances). They may attack the other's party, but never each other. In these settings, they never allow their conversation to become social, personal, or intimate. Thus, they can talk about their political passions and yet stay married by keeping their conversation in public space.

Spouses Belonging Socially

Earlier, we described social belonging as sharing "snapshots" of each other. How do husbands and wives do this? As one example, couples share social belonging in circumstances when one or both of them have to take on a new definition of who they are. This happens from the beginning. Newlyweds transform from "boyfriend" and "girlfriend" to "husband" and "wife." The baby comes and they redefine themselves as "mother" and "father." A career change prompts new definitions of self.

Such snapshots are not just definitions of self. They reflect both the stability and the changes in our lives. I have learned to nurture social belonging with my wife, Sara. She and I operate a business together. Each of us is responsible for different operations within the company. During the average day, each of us communicates significant information to another person or to other persons without sharing that communication with each other. Frequently, my administrative assistant will know before Sara does that I have scheduled an out-of-town client meeting.

Not long ago, I was in a minor traffic accident. Sara found out about it when our business partner asked, "What did you think about Joe's accident in New York?" She learned that I had seen the contrails of the ill-fated space shuttle *Columbia* when she overheard me telling my uncle over the telephone.

These events may not be matters of life and death, but such information-sharing helps keep a relationship together. When I tell others before I tell Sara, she feels as if she and I are business partners only, that she is not part of my life. Now, whenever possible, I share news with Sara before I share it with anyone else. She is my most significant connection. I want it to stay that way.

Spouses Belonging Personally

A couple belongs to each other personally when they say, "We're best friends." They share private dreams, private hopes. You can see it when a couple smiles at each other and it's obvious that there's some kind of inside joke. There is insider information that only the two of them share. And if this information were known by others they would be embarrassed.

Spouses Belonging Intimately

One might think of intimacy between couples as being limited to sex. And, yes, sex is a form of naked and not ashamed. But over time I have learned that sex and intimacy are not synonyms. In fact, married couples may need to "have sex" in all four spaces. This does not mean the couple has sexual adventures in a public park or elevator, but, that they engage each other sexually in more than one space.[8]

When someone talks to me about their waning sex life, I know that it is likely they are stuck in only one space in their relationship. Married couples need connection in all four relational spaces to experience health and satisfaction.

Intimacy between couples goes beyond the physical level. The private hopes and dreams a husband and wife share intimately are bits of information that cannot be shared safely anywhere else. They are things you would be ashamed for anyone else to know. These could be "dirty little secrets" or your weight, prescription medications, medical treatments, or dreams of grandeur. It is information you can share only with someone who won't think you're weird or crazy.

+ *Many Relationships, Four Spaces*

We've looked specifically at how husbands and wives need to belong to each other in all four spaces. By doing so, I do not mean to give the impression that marriage will meet all of our spatial belongings.

Margaret Mead describes what some expect in marriage:

> Each spouse is supposed to be all things to the other. They're supposed to be good in bed, and good out of it. Women are supposed to be good cooks, good mothers, good wives, good skiers, good conversationalists, good accountants. Neither person is supposed to find any sustenance from anybody else.[9]

This is not the spirit of what I am proposing. The pressure of trying to be all things to each other becomes overwhelming without help from other connections and from multiple spaces.

Remember Pam and Gary? As I explained the $Pu_8S_4P_2I$ ratio to Pam and Gary, I emphasized that Pam would likely be only one of Gary's public relationships. Her first response was, "I don't care who he belongs to publicly. That isn't the connection I'm looking for. In fact, he can belong to anyone he wants in all the other spaces as long as he reserves the intimate space for me."

It didn't take much discussion for Pam to recognize that her statement was not true. It *did* concern her when Gary socialized with others but didn't talk with her. She finally admitted that she *did* want to be the most significant social connection in her husband's life.

> Even under the best circumstances, marriage relies on the support of a network of friends and family. Without the ongoing involvement of outsiders, couples become isolated along with their problems, their arguments, and their misunderstandings—a situation that usually makes matters much, much worse. There's a strange contradiction between the social pressure to marry and the subsequent lack of social involvement in marriage itself. As George [a married man] observes, "There are tremendous pressures to get married ... and yet we are more atomized now. We don't have the buttressing, the support, the networks, or even the reinforcement of the shame of divorce—though that was mostly a bad thing—that helps hold people together."[10]
>
> **Pamela Paul, The Starter Marriage
> and the Future of Matrimony**

I spent time teaching both of them more about the $Pu_8S_4P_2I$ "chemical compound." Pam found comfort when she realized that she did not have to provide the entirety of Gary's communication connections. She had help.

Pam also saw that if she and Gary maintained significant connections—some of them public, some social, some personal, some intimate—between each other, she did not feel she was being replaced. This new understanding allowed Pam and Gary to begin to cultivate a healthy marriage.

+ *Forced to Move Too Far*

One of the hardest transitions in a person's life is when he or she is forced to move from one end of the spatial relational continuum to the other. This giant leap wrecks a person's search for community. This is what happens with divorce. Divorce is a move from intimate belonging to being a stranger.

After forty years of marriage, John announces to Kim that he can no longer live with her. He wants a divorce. Instantly, Kim's definition of family has changed. A most significant connection has gone from intimate to stranger. As the marriage unravels over the next several months and the divorce proceedings take place, Kim is perplexed again and again by the relationship she now holds with John. He calls her frequently to try to reach an out-of-court settlement. He wants to sell the house. Sometimes he's kind, asking about her health and well-being. Other times he's downright mean.

She hears herself saying, "This is not the man I married," or "I don't even recognize this man—he acts like a stranger."

This is not unique to Kim. Having gone through divorce myself, I know the profound sense of estrangement. The feeling of disbelief—"How could this be?"—is accompanied by confusion—"How can someone who was so close be so far away?"

Fear sets in. Our former spouse—now a stranger—has intimate knowledge about us. We were once together, naked and unashamed. Now this person has the power to destroy our public and social lives by sharing the inconsistencies, the secrets of our life. We're afraid he or she will open the closet door for all to see. We think, "Everyone will believe what they say about me."

In situations such as divorce when an intimate belonging changes, all four spaces are disrupted. If you belong only to one or two people intimately ($Pu_8S_4P_2I$) and one of them moves radically to a different space, you've just lost a significant portion of your harmonious connections.

If one space is out of harmony, all the spaces are out of harmony. You no longer have a sense that things are in place. That you belong. That you have healthy community. You question all of your relationships, all of your connections. You see how fragile all of your connections really are. And you are painfully aware that you're not in control of how others belong to you.

[
The lifeblood of relational aggression is relationship. As a result, most relational aggression occurs within intimate social or friendship networks. The closer the target to the perpetrator, the more cutting the loss. As one Linden freshman put it, "Your friends know you and how to hurt you. They know what your real weaknesses are. They know exactly what to do to destroy someone's self-worth. They try to destroy you from the inside." Such pointed meanness, an eighth grader explained to me, "can stay with you for your entire life. It can define who you are."[11]

Rachel Simmons, *Odd Girl Out:*
The Hidden Culture of Aggression in Girls
]

+ *Transitional Tension*

Dan enlisted in the army two years ago. Following boot camp he married Stephanie, his high-school sweetheart. Their daughter, Tiffany, celebrated her first birthday eighteen months later. The family has moved three times, one of which was across the country away from both of their extended families. Thus far, they've adjusted to military life well, seeing it as a big adventure.

One morning, the entire camp was called together to discuss an impending deployment to the Middle East. Spouses were invited to attend. Most of the information was routine, a review of what Dan had learned throughout his training. One piece of advice, however, caught him off guard.

"Be prepared to have a fight with your spouse the night before you ship out," the Commanding Officer stated matter-of-factly. "It's not unusual, so don't be surprised." The CO started to move to a new topic, then stopped. "Does anyone know why this happens?" he asked.

One of the wives stood. "It makes it easier to leave," she answered.

"Well done," responded the CO. "That is precisely the reason. It's easier to say good-bye when you're a little bit angry with each other. So, be prepared. This is part of going to war," the CO stressed.

Sara and I have experienced this firsthand. I was invited to spend two weeks in Kazakhstan for a mission trip. The night before I left, we had a big argument that kept us awake all night. The entire length of the fight, we both were as frustrated that we were quarreling as we were about the content of the dispute. We could not figure out why we were at odds. We discussed it over the phone as I traveled and again when I returned. In retrospect, I believe we were experiencing the transitional tension of trading spaces.

+ *Phase Transitions*

All of us recognize this formula: H_2O. But does this represent water, steam, or ice?

Water, steam, and ice have distinctive characteristics and thus their own specific definitions. The actions we take with one form of H_2O are completely different from actions we take with another form. Try to skate on a pond of water or drink a nice, cold glass of steam.

Water undergoes a *phase transition* as it moves from water to ice. During this time, H_2O is neither water nor ice. It is in fact both. The phase transitions between water and steam or water and ice hold the characteristics of both states. They could almost be given their own definitions.

The four relational spaces are much the same. There are phase transitions in moving from space to space. For example, suppose you give your mate an intimate hug while in the throes of a heated argument—a strange thing to do when the two of you are at odds. Yet such a hug could be a phase transition; it could mark the beginning of settling the issue and moving to a space where the two of you can make up.

You can probably think of relationships in your life that are more personal than most, yet not intimate. Or perhaps they are more social than personal in some contexts while being more personal than social in others. You may have a relationship that is not really personal, but it's not really social. It's kind of in between.

We flow in and out of the four spaces. We rarely make one cutting jump from here to there. When we do so, we often drag junk from one space to another. Awkwardly, we try to take our definition of belonging in one space and apply it to another. This doesn't work! You can't belong intimately to a public belonger, no matter how hard you try!

Each of the four spaces has specific parameters of action, language, and real estate. We cannot use the same definitions from one space as we enter the next. Yet, as we travel through the "betweens," this fact often gets shoved aside.

Learning the definitions and competencies of each space while at the same time knowing there is some fluidity helps us navigate through our belongings. Healthy community requires us to learn the appropriate behaviors in both the relational spaces and the gray areas between spaces.

+ So, Why Move?

Spatial phase transitions can be very confusing; often they are tense. Each party is trying to learn how to relate to the other in the new space and what adjustments may need to be made. There may even be a period of time during which neither party is sure what space the connection is in.

If transitioning is so anxiety ridden, why change the relational space? Why not eliminate the stress and keep all relationships where they are?

The Environment Has Changed

The ability to keep our relationships the same is not always within our control. Our spatial environments are in constant flux. These environmental changes necessitate movement.

It is somewhat like being at summer camp. You spend a week getting to know a few people. New friends and acquaintances have moved "closer," and those left at home for the week have been, for a short time, forgotten. Finally, it's time to go home. We promise our newfound friends that we'll never forget them and that we'll keep in touch. Yet something seems to happen during the car ride home. We do not mean to break the promise. We never expected that things would be so different once back in our everyday environment.

Fortunately, those who stayed home do not know how easily forgotten they were. We tell our "old" friends about our "new" friends. This makes the reconnection feel a little strange. Our stories do not connect. The names are unfamiliar. We find ourselves telling stories about people who are strangers to those who stayed home, which makes our resumption of our belonging more awkward and obvious.

We may have trouble overcoming this awkwardness. How do we find harmony among these belongings? Even coming home takes time.

[
Imagine walking into your favorite coffee place and ordering a double-tall latte. The person behind the counter asks how you've been, and mentions that they haven't seen you for awhile. You chat for a bit, then as they hand you your change, they ask if you'd like to "go out sometime."[12]

Linda Van Leuven, *"What Does the Service Include?"*
]

To Protect Ourselves and Others

Sometimes we trade spaces out of necessity. When Sara and I were dating, and then as newlyweds, we introduced each other to our friends and began sharing these relationships as a couple rather than as individuals. It was interesting to watch how these relationships with our own friends, and with each other's friends, changed.

Some of Sara's single friends immediately broke contact with her. Perhaps they felt they had nothing in common anymore. Another friend of hers would visit us, but would barely acknowledge my presence, even when I was in the same room! After the initial greeting, no conversation would be directed my way unless Sara initiated it. Over time, my wife pulled away from this friend.

Jane, one of my close friends, sought to develop a relationship with Sara. Jane was kind to Sara and frequently invited her out to socialize. It appeared Jane wanted to develop the same relationship with Sara—in personal space—that Jane shared with me. Sara was more than willing to do so. She liked Jane and knew that Jane and I had been friends for a long time. Sara did not want to cause any harm between Jane and me.

However, Sara soon discovered a tendency in Jane that put Sara's guard up. Whenever she was with Jane, she noticed that Jane's conversation turned against a third person. Since I was about the only person they had in common, more often than not, I was the target.

Sara decided it might be dangerous to continue a personal relationship with Jane. She could not share information with Jane in a safe place. Sara and I are still in contact with Jane, but always in social space. Trading space was necessary to protect our marriage.

To Sustain Harmony

All of us seek health. All of us constantly move relational connections seeking to keep our lives in harmony. We maintain a healthy harmony as we build significant belonging in the four spaces according to the "chemical compound" found in chapter 4 ($Pu_8S_4P_2I$).

When we move someone from one space to a space that is already "full," we frequently move someone who formerly occupied that space to another space. Many times this is only for a moment; other times for a week or month. And there are times when we move someone into a new space and keep him or her in this new space for longer periods of time.

+ *Belonging Can't Be "Processed"*

The four relational spaces are not a process for growing healthy connections. Healthy community comes when we hold harmony among the spaces. Likewise, a congregation is healthy when it promotes significant belonging in all four spaces and helps people grow in each space. Assembly line processing through the spaces is not healthy.

I presented a workshop on the language of belonging to a Midwestern audience. The next day, a young man named Mark asked if he could go to lunch with me. Mark was on staff at a megachurch in the area. I accepted his invitation.

"I've been thinking all night about the material you presented," Mark began. "This stuff has really changed my thinking on how I'm going to reorganize our small group ministry." The waiter interrupted, asking for our drink orders. As Mark looked up he realized that he knew our waiter. "Jay, how is it going? I didn't realize you had moved back to this area."

Mark and Jay shared the pleasantries common among longtime acquaintances, and then Jay hurried off to get our drinks.

"As I was saying, I have a few thoughts that I want to run by you to see what you think," Mark continued, barely slowing down long enough to breathe. "Instead of trying to get everyone to join a small group as a first step toward community, I will now help people process through the four spaces. In our worship—that's public space—we'll offer social opportunities for those who want to take the next step. Then at these social gatherings we'll encourage people to get into a small group as the next step. That gets them to personal space. In our small groups we'll encourage people to grow deeper and develop the spiritual disciplines. This gets them to intimate space. Intimate space with Christ. That's the goal. What do you think?"

"How many people would you like to see go through the process you described?" I asked.

"Everyone," Mark responded. "One hundred percent of the people in our church now and everybody we bring in. Like you said,

'Everyone seeks healthy community.'"

Jay, our waiter, was back. "Have you decided what you would like to order or do you need a few more minutes?"

Mark and I ordered, then returned to the conversation.

"So, what do you think?" asked Mark.

"Tell me about Jay."

"Our waiter? What do you want to know?"

"I noticed that the two of you know each other," I said. "Are you close? Where and when did you first meet? You know stuff like that." Mark seemed a little put off by my inquiry. Briefly he told me how he and Jay met at a weekend retreat. I could tell that Mark wanted to get back to talking about moving people through the four spaces, but I kept focusing on his relationship with Jay.

"So, have you and Jay grown close?" I asked.

"No."

"Why not?"

Mark said, "We just aren't. We never really connected anyway." He sat up straighter. "What are your thoughts about my plan?"

"Mark," I began, selecting my words carefully, "I have a puzzle for you. If you can choose how you would like to grow your relationship with Jay, why can't those who come to your church have the freedom to choose how they will grow their relationship with the congregation?"

I can see how Mark arrived at his plan. Looking at the four spaces, it does seem that people could or should "process" through them. We don't enter relationships intimately—in intimate space. Every person who ends up with an intimate connection began their relationship in another space.

So yes, there are entry points, mostly in social space. And yes, some relationships progress through the four spaces. Yet the four spaces are not an assembly line for growing community. A person cannot start at one end (public space), work through the line (the four spaces), and roll off the line a brand-new intimate belonger. We are not building cars. We are developing community among the fragile connections humans hold.

We will examine in the last chapter some ways to help people grow in each space. But for now, consider how people want and need to connect. Then help them in that space. Moving them to a different space is not always the answer.

+ *Belonging to God*

There's the question, "What about my relationship with God? I have always asserted that the relationship God demands is intimate."

Me too!

I was taught that God yearns to return to the "Eden" relationship. For years I believed that. Everything God has done is an effort to reconcile us to him.

I had always believed that the relationship he desired was intimate. I've lived my life trying to connect intimately with God. There have been some moments when I have experienced the overwhelming intimate presence of the Almighty in my life, but much of the time has been spent trying to get to the mountain.

Until I embarked on the journey to describe how people grew healthy community in their lives, I had never thought it could be any different. In fact, because of my conservative religious upbringing, I felt guilty most of my life knowing that I had experienced intimacy with God very few times. Don't get me wrong. I have experienced God in my life many times. I know that he is involved in my walk through life. But intimately? Rarely.

Can belonging to God be public and healthy? Can I be a social belonger to the Maker of the universe?

Historically, churches have promoted *personal* and *intimate* as the preferred spaces to belong. But if a person belongs to God in a public or social way, is it up to us to "correct" it? Is it wrong to help people grow their public relationship without requiring them to grow it "closer" in a different space?

These are difficult questions.

"Can a Fool Be Saved?"

I was saved, I think, at a gospel revival at the Green Lake Bible camp two summers ago after a sermon by Brother Fred Rowley, who preached about the ship *Titanic* and the tycoons and society ladies on board who paid little heed to Spiritual Things and devoted themselves to Worldly Pleasures and suddenly, in the midst of their glittering evening of Glamour and Elegance, them in their tuxedos and evening gowns sipping their champagne and discussing the wonderful fun they'd have when they docked in New York City, the parties, the dinners— suddenly came a horrendous CRACKING and CRUNCHING and GROANING and SHRIEKING from the bowels of the "unsinkable" ship and the roar of seawater and a few hours later they plunged to their deaths in the frigid Atlantic, their souls sinking into an Eternity of Darkness without God. And I sat in my seat, trembling, thinking that if God could sink an ocean liner, He could easily drop a meteor on our house or blow up the furnace or poison the water or arrange for a gunman to come and murder us in our beds, as the choir sang, "I've wandered far away from God, now I'm coming home. The paths of sin too long I've trod. Lord, I'm coming home." And I said, "Come into my heart, Lord Jesus."

But was that enough?

Brother Rowley said anyone who wanted to accept Jesus Christ as Saviour should come forward—and I didn't go. I preferred to be saved sitting quietly in my seat. I didn't care to be a tree toad on his knees, bawling, for everyone to gawk at. So I sat in my seat and quietly invited Jesus into my heart. But did He come in? Or did He say, "If you're too scared to come down front, then why should I walk all the way back there?"

Condemned to eternal perdition because I was too shy to walk fifty feet! What a fool![13]

Garrison Keillor, *Lake Wobegon Summer 1956*

We Are Not in Control

We are not in control of who belongs to us; neither are we in control of who belongs to God. Belonging to the kingdom is a God decision. The Gospels often reflect Jesus asking—even warning—us not to make kingdom decisions.

In the parable of the weeds[14] the servants seek permission to cleanse the field of the weeds. The response is an emphatic, "No." The reason given was that the owner of the field is afraid that the servants may uproot the wheat. In other words, the servants may not know the difference between wheat and weeds. The servants are told that the decision will be made at the harvest.

In the parable of the net[15] the kingdom is likened to gathering good and bad fish in the same throw of the net. Again, the separation is left to the angels and occurs at the harvest, not during the catch.

Parable after parable emphasizes that we have little knowledge of who belongs. It's often those we would not expect to belong: children, prostitutes, tax collectors, and drunkards. In Matthew 25, both the sheep and the goats ask the same question: "Lord, when did we see you . . . ?"[16] Neither group knows who belongs and who doesn't.

In the parable of the prodigal son, one son dutifully worked on the farm. The other son was irresponsible and squandered his inheritance. It looks as if the son who stayed had the intimate relationship with the father. Yet by the end of the story we realize that the older son was probably farther away from his father than the prodigal.

> The older brother became angry and refused to go in. So his father went out and pleaded with him. But he answered his father, "Look! All these years I've been slaving for you and never disobeyed your orders. Yet you never gave me even a young goat so I could celebrate with my friends. But when this son of yours who has squandered your property with prostitutes comes home, you kill the fattened calf for him!"
> "My son'" the father said, "you are always with me, and everything I have is yours. But we had to celebrate and be glad, because this brother of yours was dead and is alive again; he was lost and is found."[17]

Even in the far country, the prodigal knew he could come back. He knew that he could enjoy the family connection, even if it were as a slave. The older son never knew that. Yet both sons belonged to the family.

Jesus Is Comfortable in All Four Spaces

When we look through Jesus' relationships, we find that he is comfortable having people belong in multiple ways. In chapter 3, we mentioned the centurion.[18] Jesus not only is comfortable with the soldier belonging in a public space, but he points to the centurion's faith as exemplary.

Gethsemane is another place that clearly shows Jesus' ability to have diverse, significant spatial belonging. Jesus took his disciples to Gethsemane to pray. He said to them, "'Sit here while I go over there and pray.' He took Peter and the two sons of Zebedee along with him, and he began to be sorrowful and troubled. Then he said to them, 'My soul is overwhelmed with sorrow to the point of death. Stay here and keep watch with me.' Going a little farther, he fell with his face to the ground and prayed."[19]

He left the whole group, took Peter, James, and John, then left them to go to an intimate place with God. Some of Jesus' disciples belonged in a different space than did others. Jesus seemed comfortable with their belonging in the space of their choosing.

Many belonged to Jesus in different spaces. The Bible mentions the multitudes, a room full, a crowd of seventy, twelve apostles, the inner circle of Peter, James, and John. All experienced community with Jesus.

What would this look like in our congregations and communities? Are we comfortable with people belonging to Jesus and the church in public or social space? Can we give them significant connections in whatever space they choose to belong without pushing them to come closer?

Jesus never forced strangers to become intimate. Instead he encouraged them to move from stranger to public belonger. "I was a stranger and you invited me in," does not imply intimacy. The stranger is invited in, to belong publicly.

+ *Moving Day*

When Sara and I decided to move from an apartment to a house, we excluded certain parts of town and listed features we did *not* need in our new home. We found this to be more useful than making a list of requirements.

I find the same kind of list—the don'ts—helpful in trading relational spaces. We need to be able to recognize when we or when others use space inappropriately so that we can move ourselves or move others to a space that would bring harmony.

What are some inappropriate ways we use space to belong? I use photographs to illustrate how people prepare space and use space to promote a specific kind of connection. In my travels I have taken a lot of pictures, and I enjoy showing these photos to groups and having the group choose what space is being promoted in the photo. Then I ask if this is an effective use of visual space for making the anticipated connection.

One particular photo always produces confusing and conflicting answers. I took a picture in Chicago of a homeless man sleeping on a concrete walkway in a public park. The viewers always grapple over whether that is public space or intimate space. What the group finally comes to is that the man is using the public space inappropriately. I've noticed that the man's inappropriate use of space upsets the group as much as his poverty.[20]

Space can be used inappropriately because of cultural norms. We readily see this when we travel abroad. The rules of engagement are diverse. In our culture we shake hands, which is offensive in some cultures. Some bow or kiss, awkward customs to us. In North America when we meet someone, we tend to pass—even when walking—on the right. Try this in England and you bump into people. You soon find out how strange you are when you use spatially specific actions in the wrong place.

Visiting one of the fastest growing churches in the United States, I entered the worship center with great anticipation. The first thing I noticed was the lighting. The stage was well lit, but the seating area was dark. The worship started with a strong, well-performed song. Then we were asked to stand and join in if we wanted to for the second song. Most stood but just watched. When the second song was over, the host asked us to turn and greet the people around us. Wow, did that feel out of place.

I've been in several services where this kind of social introduction was a part of the liturgy, but it felt different here. Through the announcement time and the first part of the sermon, I tried to figure out what felt so strange about the "shaking hands" event. Then I remembered how dark it was. Darkness creates an environment of anonymity. We couldn't see each other. The darkness transformed the seating area into very public space. Our only visual contact was with those on stage, and it was doubtful they could see us.

When we were asked to "Shake hands and say 'Hi,'" it was almost like walking up to a stranger at night and putting out your hand. The space was too dark for us to act in what was meant to be a typically appropriate social way.

When I travel on business, I can tell what the flight will be like by the way the person in the next seat tries to engage me in conversation. If that person doesn't seem too curious or doesn't exchange a simple greeting, I know I can relax. However, if the person tries to begin a friendly chat, I know I am probably in for a long ride and usually a neck ache by the time we land.

Commercial airplanes are public space. The seating is not arranged for comfortable social interaction. Even though you are seated shoulder-to-shoulder, the seating arrangement forces everyone to look straight ahead with limited eye contact with other passengers. It is inappropriate to engage someone in social intercourse on an airplane.

This is not to say that I have no interest in my fellow passengers. Sometimes I notice the title of a book someone is reading, and I ask about their interest in the topic. But when I do so, I am aware that I have crossed the line and I tread lightly and politely. Many times I will actually stand in the aisle and then engage in conversation. We can then both comfortably converse.

Most passengers sit quietly and keep to themselves until landing. At landing and while the plane taxis to the gate, it seems appropriate to trade some pleasantries. I believe this is accepted because the trip has almost ended and you feel like you will not get trapped in a long conversation. Everyone knows the conversation will be short.

Inappropriate belonging also occurs when people know how to connect in only one space. I am friends with two well-known members of the speaking circuit who meet hundreds of people over the course of a year. The first time someone meets either of these headliners, the individual believes he has just become the speaker's personal friend. It doesn't take long before the individual realizes that the "personal connection" wasn't so personal at all. They feel disillusioned, hurt, and used.

The truth is that my friends have not used anyone. They simply have not developed the competencies necessary to engage people in social space.

+ *Learning to Trade Spaces*

Now that we know where we don't want to move to—or move others to—we must ask: How do we trade spaces? A move is always stressful, even one that is planned. Packing up, throwing out. Pushing forward and holding on. An unexpected move can be devastating.

Have you ever watched a family move an unsuspecting elderly parent into a care facility? Or maybe you or someone you know has been burned out of their home. The space called *home* is quickly changed to something else.

Moving or helping others move from one relational space to another takes care. We must do so with the grace of our Lord. Jesus moves people to different spatial relationships. He gives a wonderful example of this as he's dying on the cross.

> Near the cross of Jesus stood his mother, his mother's sister, Mary the wife of Clopas, and Mary Magdalene. When Jesus saw his mother there, and the disciple whom he loved standing nearby, he said to his mother, "Dear woman, here is your son," and to the disciple, "Here is your mother." From that time on, this disciple took her into his home.[21]

Why did he do that on the cross? He knew he was coming back. Why didn't he help her trade spaces at a less tragic time? Clearly, Jesus wanted Mary's physical needs taken care of. But I believe he was also taking care of her spatial needs. He was saying, "From now on, I'm not going to be able to provide this kind of spatial connection." In this tender moment, he was moving Mary to a space where she would have her needs met. From now on, John would be that person for her.

> All the miseries of Scrooge's unreconstructed life in Dickens's "A Christmas Carol," that best known of Christmas books, lead up to this great misery: that he sees himself dying alone and unmourned. This is the time of year when solitude is feared most, when the human community labors, in all kinds of ways, to bring stragglers under its great wing. [22]
>
> **Anna Quindlen, "Begone, Buzz! Be Still, Soul"**

People give us the gift of relational space. They want to connect and they give clues to how they would like to connect. If we try to connect in a different way, the person may feel attacked or unwanted.

May we learn to "read" the space that people invite us into. May we be at peace with whatever space people want to connect with us. We can have significant belonging in whatever space people invite us into.

May we be sensitive to the needs of those around us, sometimes moving ourselves—sometimes helping others move—to a space more comfortable, more harmonious and healthy.

+ [*consider*]

+ What has been the most difficult spatial transition you
  have had to make? What were some of the emotions you
  experienced?

+ When thinking through the spatial transitions you have made,
  what helpful discoveries come to mind as you assist others
  connecting with your congregation?

+ Have you experienced the four spatial belongings in your relationships with God? Your family? Your mate?

+ What competencies do you have for transitioning spatial
  belonging? What competency would you like to add? In your
  church, what congregational competencies are apparent for
  spatial transition?

+ When helping others with their community puzzle, how much
  of the puzzle is caused by trading spaces? How can you help?

searching for a front porch

Nobody thought much about the front porch when most Americans
had them and used them. The great American front porch was just
there, open and sociable, an unassigned part of the house that belonged to everyone
and no one, a place for family and friends to pass time.[1]

Rochlin, "The Front Porch," *in* **Home Sweet Home**

I
t was a long, late spring day. I arrived home just as the sun
was returning to the other side for the night. I parked my
car on the street in front of my house, locked the door, swung my
computer bag over my shoulder, and headed up the driveway trying
to shed the troubles of the day. My stroll was interrupted by a voice
from across the street.

"How was your day?" It was Tom Donelan.

"It went well," I turned and replied.

"It sure is a nice evening."

"Yes," I replied and then I continued toward the front door.

It is a reassuring peace to know that the Donelans will be on
their front porch enjoying the evening. I am always quite envious. I
would love to have a front porch. Their home is the only one on our
street that has one. Most of our homes sport a wood deck on the
back, yet the Donelans' front porch makes this street seem more
neighborly, secure, and serene.

Walking to the door, my mind races to my childhood. I remember the great times I had playing on my great-grandparents' big farmhouse front porch. I remember one of my favorite TV shows as a child, now in reruns, *The Andy Griffith Show*. Watching Andy, Barney, Opie, and Aunt Bea relaxing for the evening on their front porch made the world seem right.

[
Mama used to roll her hair
Back before the central air.
We'd sit outside and watch the stars at night.
She'd tell me to make a wish
I'd wish we both could fly.
Don't think she's seen the sky
Since we got the satellite dish.[2]

James McMurtry, "Levelland," *Where'd You Hide the Body?*
]

I wish for a front porch. I am not alone. In our time people have a hunger for a significant "median space." This may arise from the recent history of minimizing the importance of these relationships. Median spaces are the spaces that include our social and personal connections. Median spaces are where people experience "front porch." Front porches are significant to our experience of community and belonging.

The American front porch further represented the ideal of community in America. For the front porch existed as a zone between the public and private, an area that could be shared between the sanctity of the home and the community outside. It was an area where interaction with the community could take place. For "the master's farm business, the mistress's selections of goods and produce, the home craftsmen's sales, and sundry negotiations of the cooler sort (with the hired man, the foreman, the slave or house servant, the distressed or disgruntled neighbor, even with the unpredictable stranger from the muddy road) could all be conducted in the civil atmosphere offered by the shade of a prominent porch, apart from the sleeping and feeding quarters and without serious risk to the family's physical and psychic core" (Out on the Porch). The porch further fostered a sense of community and neighborliness. In the evenings, as people moved outdoors, the porch served to connect individuals. The neighbors from next door might stop by one's house, to sit on the porch and discuss both personal and community issues. The couple walking down the street might offer a passing "hello," as they passed house after house whose inhabitants rested outdoors.[3]

Where have the front porches gone? How can we spot them? How can we develop them in our congregations, in our human relationships, and with God?

+ A Short History of Space

In the '40s and '50s we were on the move. The roar of the wars and the crash of the market had taken their toll on the family, and we were rebuilding. A swift move to planned communities surrounding the fulcrum industry "saved" us from the family farm. Soldiers came home to build new, safe lives. White picket fences claimed the ground for the newly constructed suburban culture. City dwellings and family farms were abandoned to build a community called *neighborhood*. Neighborhoods grew strong, the suburbs sprawled, and social connection was at a high.

[
But there is one more key factor: you must have social interaction to have a true place. Many suburbs stymied social interaction by physically fragmenting our lives. Our homes, jobs, shopping, entertainment, houses of worship, and civic institutions were all separated from each other. In effect, most suburbs became the antithesis of true places.[4]

Charles C. Bohl, *Place Making: Developing Town Centers, Main Streets, and Urban Villages*
]

The term "bedroom community" described the phenomenon of the separation of work and home. For the first time we lived closer to work than to family. Sidewalks gave way to center turn lanes, and dating moved "from front porch to back seat" (the title of a book by Beth L. Bailey).

As we spent more time at the workbench than around the dining room table, our personal and intimate connections slowly changed. We experienced a pervasive disconnect with our traditional family relationships and turned inward to find the answer. We searched for the significance that was once experienced through the family tree.

Stirring underground was the equal rights movement. The desire for equitable living and opportunity forced us to assess everyone's potential in this new world. Communities reviewed boundaries, and the picket fences began to come down.

We rode the waves of an economic movement. We went from the economic structure of the Industrial Age to the speed-driven Information Age. The hard, cold data ushered in the "high touch" service economy. Then we searched for more than service and discovered that it was "the experience" that sells. And now we are watching the birth of the fuzzy, relational economy. Product to data, data to service, service to experience, and now, we buy connection.

Architecture traveled alongside. The view of the handcrafted farmhouse was obscured by the "instant" construction of prefabricated homes. Television and air conditioning defaced our neighborhoods— front porches were no longer needed. Downtown shops were replaced by strip malls. Strip malls were covered and the modern indoor-shopping experience was born. "Green space" entered our vocabulary. Driving replaced walking. Mom and Pop fell to franchise. And now, franchise shares market with specialty.

The Hide-and-Seek City

The profession of city planning emerged out of landscape architecture during the first two decades of the twentieth century, and by the mid-1930s most American cities had a planning department. Building codes, fire districts, and acceptable standards for everything from gas and electric lines to street widths became typical by the 1930s. In addition, banks and savings and loan institutions developed standardized procedures for property appraisal as well as commonly accepted ideas about what types of structures and spaces to encourage or discourage. Single-family houses, for example, were seen in a positive light, but residential hotels were frowned upon. Similarly, curvilinear residential streets were good, but alleys were bad. Front porches were an unnecessary expense and could easily be eliminated, but garages and driveways were essential. Corner stores were also discouraged on a number of counts: they mixed residential and commercial activities together and often had inadequate off-street parking. Every planner and lender gradually learned the rules. With the establishment of the Federal Housing Authority in the mid-1930s, planning and lending practices standardized, eliminating many of the interesting quirks of the traditional city. . . .

Beyond basic safety regulations, the justification for expanding codes was usually the protection of property values. The pessimistic view of society maintained that people had to be protected from one another. In residential areas, it was thought that, given the chance, some people would immediately paint their houses hideous colors and find abandoned trailers to put in weed-filled front yards. If corner stores and small parks were provided, they would only attract undesirables who hang out and cause trouble. If front porches were built, nosy neighbors could spy on others and, worse yet, bother people. On-street parking and narrow streets would lead to accidents, vandalism, ugly oil spots, and other problems. A grid pattern of streets would invite speeding traffic and strangers into the neighborhood, and if alleys were provided, unimaginable evils would likely abound there. Gradually, the typical house became more isolated, introverted, and fortresslike. The facade came to be dominated by massive, perpetually closed garage doors and paved driveways. The cul-de-sac became the location of choice. These trends often resulted in the demise of the gregarious house . . .

The pessimistic view of human nature and the associated dislike of ad hoc public spaces has led to what I call the hide-and-seek city, wherein houses and apartments provide isolated, defensive places for people to hide from the rigors of urban life. Gated communities at the end of cul-de-sacs are examples of the more extreme versions of the phenomenon. Residents hiding in such refuges must deliberately seek out other dimensions of urban life by making long, often boring trips to major, enclosed, self-contained attractions. The trip likely consists of getting into a car in the garage at home and getting out in the garage of the final destination. Between the two poles, very little life exists in the ordinary spaces between buildings.[5]

Larry R. Ford, *The Spaces between Buildings*

All this was fertile ground for the self-help movement, which assisted us in discovering our intimate selves. The self-help movement fed an individualistic consumer movement. We grew in our awareness of individual needs and wants. The promise and hope was that knowing ourselves would prepare us to have healthy connections with each other since individually we were now healthier.

We explored intimate health through self-help books and gathering in small "help groups." We were encouraged to share our innermost thoughts and to discuss our struggles with our demons. "Intimacy" was fostered as the most significant way to experience health. The search for community could now be reconstructed because we had found the close connections we lost and now connected to nonfamily on a "deeper" plane.

The church growth movement courted the small group movement. Self-help groups became the model for religious home-cell groups. Accountability, exclusivity, and obligatory involvement were the pillars for growth. "Forced belonging" promised community, individual growth, and additional numbers to the church rolls.

Somewhere along the way we lost our extended families, and our public and social connections could not sustain the community conversation. Our search for community swiftly swung to paying full attention to personal and intimate space (Figure 1).

We searched for *"a place where everybody knows your name."*

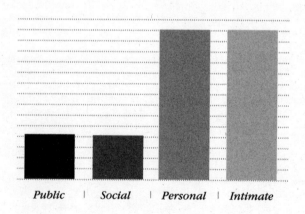

Public | Social | Personal | Intimate

Figure 1

Societies and clubs gained strong growth in membership and, along with the church, were slowly moving from social gathering place to a place to find the "family" we had moved away from. Phrases such as "personal Lord and Savior" became the secret handshake. We were searching for the intimate connections of the family farm, the family church, and the family album.

As we distilled personal and intimate health to simple steps and procedures, the church growth movement slowly followed suit. Finding family could now be accomplished in twelve, or thirty, or eight easy steps. This model lured the church into believing that a community could be developed with a good business plan. "A few simple steps and you're on your way to becoming a strong 'foster' home."

The Search for Excellent Space

But something did not quite ring true. We were building cars and churches with the same plan. And both were feeling the effects of the incestuous preoccupation we had with ourselves. Although the church was "discipling deep-rooted followers," it was not effective in reaching the community. The church lost touch with its neighbors, and fewer numbers of people believed it had a relevant message.

The church followed the same path as the big-three car manufacturers, which experienced market loss. Although we were paying incredible attention to ourselves, we were building an inferior product. The assembly lines were occupied by individuals; yet it takes a team to build an automobile.

The Japanese, being "behind the times," exploded into the market. It was not about personal and intimate health to them. It is the public that consumes the product. Loyalty lost its luster. "Built in the USA" could no longer separate the buyer from his cash. It was a new day and *The Search for Excellence* craze ushered in the service economy. It was time to look outside ourselves and pay close attention to the end user. The consumer became king.

The church claimed its hold on the service community by announcing that it is the place to find true service. We refocused our plan and built a worship experience that serviced the needs of unchurched "Harry." A full band replaced the organ. Hymns were swapped for choruses. Contemplative and liturgical worship was replaced by lively celebrations. Celebratory worship sought to entice "Harry and Harriet" to return. "It is about them," we proudly exclaimed. Anonymity and freedom of choice became the rule for community development.

"Public space" was a marketing strategy and "seeker-sensitive" became the buzz. Weekend services were entirely developed for "them." Expository sermons became felt-need stories. A list of helpful workshop suggestions littered the bulletin. Monetary giving and committed involvement were discouraged as inappropriate behavior for a "visitor." We took every step to develop a space where strangers could "come and see."

We built services for members during the midweek, and the chasm between "us" and "them" deepened. You are either in one space or another—public or intimate (Figure 2). It is plain to see who is a part of the family and who is just passing through.

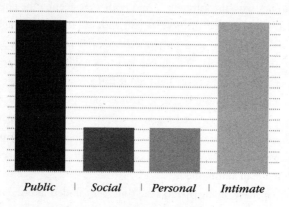

Public | Social | Personal | Intimate

Figure 2

So, here we are still circling the original questions: How do we invite strangers into the family? How can we help with the experience of belonging? How do we develop healthy community? I believe the answers may be found somewhere in the median spaces—somewhere on the front porch. But where can we find these treasures of community?

+ Bob Marley Invites Me to His Front Porch: An American Jewel Returns

I was enjoying my stroll up Broadway. The bright lights, the sea of people, and the melodies of car horns embellish the play that is Broadway. Against this background was the least likely place I thought I would discover an old American treasure.

I was waiting for the light to change at 51st Street so I could continue my pleasant journey. As I waited, I looked to see what surprises might lie ahead. There on the corner was an archeological find. It is no wonder I had not seen it before. It did not look the same. Time had allowed it to morph into something shaped far different from its ancestors. There on the corner of 51st and Broadway was the reemergence of the American front porch. Maybe it never went away. If not, it has been in hiding.

What really tuned my eye to this find was the invitation written on the billboard above the door. With a photo of Bob Marley in the background it read:

One love, one heart.
Let's get together and feel all right.
Give thanks and praise to the Lord and I will feel all right.
Let's get together and feel all right.[6]

As I looked below the massive invitation, I saw several people peering out of a window. They were seated along a bar facing out and warming their hands around a cup of designer "joe." What the billboard was inviting us to was to join the community on the front porch—it was inviting us into Starbucks.

It is true that the front porch has disappeared from many of our homes. However, this median space has not disappeared from our culture. We need this space, and so we have built it elsewhere. Places like Starbucks provide a new front porch experience. Such places have experienced success for more reasons than just their unique blends of coffee. It is the experience of social connection that draws people to stop in for a moment.

> One of the things I wanted to talk about in this movie was the idea of the third place, which is Ray Oldenburg's theory of how everyone needs a third place—your home, your office, and the third place. Of course Starbucks—one of the reasons it's so successful—is that it's such a pleasant third place, among others (God knows other places that are great third places). I actually have a theory that one of the reasons crime is down in the cities is because there are so many Starbucks, and they all have windows with people sitting in them, looking out at the street. And as we know, when people are watching the street, there's less crime. It's my own little theory and probably is not true, but, there you go.[7]
>
> **Nora Ephron, Director, *You've Got Mail***

There is a new shopping center near our home in which the shops range from designer clothing to a health food market. It is wildly popular. It has experienced a great deal of success—even more than the malls in our town. It is hard to understand why. All of the shops are built on the old "strip mall" concept. This is a good concept for warmer climates, but in Cincinnati? It gets very cold and oppressively hot here much of the year. So why is it more popular than the nearby enclosed mall? How do they get consumers to brave the elements to browse the establishments?

> [I]f the only reason people come there is to shop, then the project has fallen short of creating the type of magnetic destination where people go to become engaged in the community and to experience the place itself.[8]
>
> **Charles C. Bohl, *Place Making: Developing Town Centers, Main Streets, and Urban Village***

The answer: Most people don't go there to shop! I certainly don't.

When the architects designed the experience, they were very careful to invite the correct "anchor" stores. In the nearby mall they have department stores such as J.C. Penney's and Sears to anchor the shopping experience. The new center features trendier shops–Gap,

Cold Water Creek, and Anthropologie—but these are not the anchors.

The anchors are trendy, medium-scale restaurants. Max and Erma's, Bucca De Beppo, and P.F. Chang's provide the reason for people to show up. All of them provide the new environment for front porch to be experienced in our communities.

When I want to get together with friends, I don't invite them over. We go to a neutral place—a median space. These places provide the space between public and intimate. They provide the space for "personal and community" discussions. They provide front porch.

[[F]ew organized groups advocate neighborhood sociability....
informal spaces or "nooks and crannies" of spontaneous daily life.[9]

Larry R. Ford, *The Spaces between Buildings*]

When my neighbor knocks on my front door, I answer. What comes next creates a dilemma. I have to make a decision. I can decide to invite him in, join him on the front lawn, or stand leaning, halfway in and halfway out. It feels way too close to invite him in. If I join him on the lawn, it prompts the question, "Why didn't he invite me in?" If I stand with one foot in and one foot out it seems rude. I communicate that I haven't any time to spend, and he soon moves on. In the absence of the front porch, we have no appropriate space to converse.

Similarly, my wife and I rarely invite others over to our house to eat. We are not alone in this. Many no longer feel comfortable offering this social invitation. We do not have the time or interest to keep up the house as our grandparents did. And many have not furnished their homes to provide social interaction. Most homes have intimate spaces and public spaces. There are intimate spaces such as the bedroom and bathroom. The rooms we usually call family rooms are really designed around the viewing pleasure of watching TV. This is a public space. And most dining rooms are left unused. But have we stopped eating with friends? No. We meet them in places that provide front porch experiences.

In our time we search for significant connections on the front porch. Our culture is ready for organizations to provide space where social and personal connections can develop in healthy ways. This is not in the absence of the other spaces. It is in harmony with them.

+ *Shopping or Dating?*

The cultural trend to seek out front porch is evident in the phenomenon of "church shopping." For several years, we have credited consumerism with birthing the trend for people to "shop" for a church that offers a buffet of choices to meet their many needs. We have observed many individuals jumping denominational lines. We attributed these evils to the consumer mentality of our time. Yet I am not convinced this is at the heart of people's search.

There may be several fundamental life searches, but the search to consume is not among them. People consume in an effort to fulfill a search. For example, a person may purchase a new outfit to help with their search for identity and individuality. At the same time another may make the same purchase to quench a desire to fit in, which helps with their search to belong. People do not consume just to consume.

What I believe may be happening is that people are dating our congregations. They are looking for communities where they can become a part of the family. You do not shop for family. You date to find family.

How do we help with this dating relationship? One way may be to provide the appropriate space for dating. In days gone by, the primary space for dating was the front porch. This is because it provided a space that was far enough away from the rest of the family that the couple could get to know one another. Yet it was close enough to the family that the relationship was kept in check. It is also true that the front porch provided a space where the neighbors could see but could not interrupt. This median space was an appropriate space to date.

We now see a young man arrive at the front door and quickly drive off with his date seated beside him in his car. We have moved the dating space from front porch to back seat. We expect two developing young adults (teens) to enter a car and act as though it were the front porch. A car is an intimate space to most Americans. It is really an inappropriate space to date.

Likewise, I find congregations asking those who show up for their first date to drive off with them to an unknown destination. And, unfortunately, many times we ask them to enter intimate space to experience real church, the real God, real community, real belonging, and real love. I warn my teenage daughter against dates that promote such empty, manipulative promises.

> While the advice literature itself worked to place courtship in the public realm, its content (and, indeed, the entire public discourse on courtship) contained contradictory messages about the proper relationship between the public and the private.... Many experts insisted that the "private" sphere of courtship should provide a safe zone—a respite from the too-rapid social and cultural changes taking place between men and women in the "public" world of work.[10]
>
> **Beth L. Bailey, *From Front Porch to Back Seat: Courtship in Twentieth-Century America***

Developing a front porch to your congregation's house of belonging may help those who come hoping for a good date with the promise of a good family.

+ *Building Front Porches*

After the worship service was over, I noticed a line forming. It stretched from the atrium through the double doors into the back of the sanctuary. The vestibule was large and had a glass wall that extended from floor to ceiling. However, it was empty save the line.

I entered the line watching people patiently waiting to greet the pastor. There was limited interaction. It felt a little like the procession in a cafeteria restaurant. Thankfully, it moved quickly.

I had heard that this congregation was very friendly and had built a solid experience of community. I had yet to see evidence of this. However, upon my exit I discovered a mall of activity. People were standing around outside laughing, children running and chasing, and all in all having a good time. What I had stumbled upon was the community porch. The atrium housed the line. The patio housed the community.

Building environments can affect belonging and community. Take for example the typical church building atrium. Most atriums were built to act as people movers. They do not promote the space for people to connect in.

[

Visit www.hellomynameisscott.com

Scott Ginsberg, A Practical Way to Create Personal Front Porches

]

It is essential in our culture for churches to provide a space that develops front porch experiences. Both the architecture of our buildings and the framework of our programs can provide these spaces. Offering opportunities where people can connect and grow socially helps provide this experience. Many congregations offer these kinds of "get togethers." However most of them have some sort of relational string attached to them.

This feels like those "free" vacation offers I receive from telemarketers. You get free accommodations at a resort if you will agree to sit through a sales presentation. After arriving you are made to feel guilty if you do not take the opportunity they are offering you. Many of our "come and see" social gatherings are infested with some of the same dynamics.

To effectively create a front porch experience, there cannot be any expectations that the group would, should, or could move from social space into a different relational space. Social space is where individuals may decide to move to a different space. But it is not a space that congregations should use as a means to the end of getting people to move. Let people move themselves. Don't insist on doing it for them.

+ *Andy's Porch*

When I think of trying to build healthy front porch experiences I look to Andy for help. *The Andy Griffith Show* supplied some of the best examples of healthy median space. On Andy's front porch there was peaceful relaxation after a meal prepared by Aunt Bea. There were times filled with playing the guitar and singing. There were times for courting Helen. And sometimes there were strong words of discipline for Opie. We can build all of these into the front porches we create.

Front porches provide opportunities for fun and relaxation, worship and discipline. These are the spaces where people come to find out what our family is all about. These are the spaces where individuals come to grow and develop relationships. These are the spaces people come for a good date and expect to court and be courted. In our time front porches provide a key to helping individuals with their search for healthy community and belonging.

+ [*consider*]

+ What socially accepted rules are followed on a front porch?
+ Do you have a comfortable front porch area for people to connect in? Does your congregation?
+ Define or describe what a good date would be between your congregation and someone seeking to connect.
+ Where are the front porches in your community? Does your congregation have any connection with these? Should it?

[*seven*]

what now?
finding harmony

Tuesday, 3:30 p.m.

"Joe Myers, please."

"This is Joe. Can I help you?"

"It's good to reach you," the caller began, speaking rapidly. "My name's Kendall, and I'm pastor of First Church. I'm calling to see if I could get some information about the language of belonging."

I had never met Kendall nor had I ever been in his city.

"Sure," I said to him. "But first, how did you get my name and how did you become aware of the language of belonging?"

"It's a little complicated," he said. "A few months ago our elders' board and I came to the conclusion that we were spending a lot of time and money trying to develop a small group ministry. We weren't cutting it. We needed to do something.

"Eight years ago we committed ourselves to become a church built around small groups. We looked around until we found the best small group pastor we could find and we hired him."

"Okay," I responded, forming the picture in my mind.

He continued, "For the first month, I preached a series on how true community comes from small groups. I took examples from some of the bigger churches and showed how small groups are the key to their success. We did two training sessions, each one with a meal, a question-and-answer time afterward, and a time to sign up."

"How did it go?" I asked.

"We were thrilled!" he told me. Then he added, "Nothing in this place had been so well planned in a long time. You could just feel everybody's expectations."

I waited. "And——?"

I could hear him take a breath. "Well, that was eight years ago." He paused again. "We've had some successes. People have been helped. But not nearly what we hoped for. Not even close to what was promised. And what's worse, things have gotten a little ugly."

"What happened?" I thought I could see it coming.

"Our small group pastor left," he began. "He didn't just leave; we had to ask him to go. That's been hard. We've got a couple of hard-core small groups that are upset over his leaving. Some of the others are in the wait-and-see mode."

I raised a question: "So you still have several small groups, even though he is not there now?"

"Yes," Kendall responded. "But now we've got to do something. Here's our situation: Is the answer to bring on another small group pastor? We had one, and frankly, we were underwhelmed. Was it the pastor? Or is it the small group model?"

Kendall continued, "That's when I started searching the Web, and I came across your Web page.[1] I tried every key word dealing with small groups, church growth, community, belonging, and so on. Almost every site promoted the same stuff we had just spent eight years doing.

"That wasn't all I discovered. I was surprised at the way everybody defined their success. They all aimed for 100 percent involvement but showed only about 30 percent fulfillment. We were doing that, and it sure didn't feel like success. Yours was different. It looks to us like your site can give us some answers."

Now it was my turn to take a breath. I asked, "How can I help?"

"Well, I printed everything I could off your Web site and read through it. I read it over and over again the next couple of days. I read it to my wife. We talked about it. I read it to Tom, a friend of mine. My son is in divinity school and I called him.

"When the night came for me to make a recommendation to our board about the future of our small group ministry, I read your stuff to them. We had quite a discussion. Things got late, but nobody wanted to go home. We kept getting new ideas. I don't think any of us wanted to leave until we had made some kind of decision."

I didn't say anything, but I was powerfully interested in what would come next.

"It was obvious we would never go back to the same old small group model. But what to do? When we took a vote, it was unanimous. We were dismantling the small group ministry."

Kendall sounded like someone who had just made a confession. Then he asked, "So, I've come to you—now what?"

I swallowed hard, then asked, "Have you announced your decision?"

"No. We plan to do that Sunday. Make the announcement and field a few questions."

I knew my response would be a challenge for him: "First, let me suggest that you not make that announcement on Sunday."

"Not make the announcement?" Kendall asked.

"Let's lay that aside for a bit," I suggested. "Help me puzzle through the way your church promotes community across the entire congregation. Let's do that before we start throwing things out."

"Okay," he responded, slightly less anxious than before. Silence for a few moments, then he said, "This is going in a much different direction than I thought it would. I hope you're right. But I need to make a few calls to our elder board to slow down the announcement. Then could I call you back?"

We agreed to talk later that evening for the first of what was to become months of conversations.

Tuesday, 9:55 p.m.

"Joe? This is Kendall. Sorry to call so late."

"So, how did your board take the news?" I asked.

"To my surprise they were all relieved." Kendall continued. "After the meeting and the vote, they went home to tell their spouses the news. To a person they all ran headfirst into a wall of resistance. This made them leery about Sunday's announcement."

At least one hurdle was crossed. "I'm glad to hear everyone is in agreement about postponing the decision," I told him, feeling a great deal of relief myself.

Kendall wanted more. "So now what? How can we build 'healthy community,' as you call it? How can we help individuals with their 'search to belong'?"

Even though he was using my words—and if he had read my site as often as he claimed, he must have said the words over and over—for some reason the way he spoke them made them sound alien to me.

Kendall's call came just a couple of days after the Web site went live. I had put some of my rough ideas there to see if I could get a response that would lead to a discussion of healthy community. I did not expect anyone to take my Web site as a model for their church's future.

I decided to be open with him. "Kendall," I said, "I am somewhat anxious about your willingness to take this idea hook, line, and sinker. I have just started working through these ideas myself. I'm not yet aware of all the implications."

But Kendall was more ready than I was. "Joe," he said, "all I can tell you is that our leaders found that your material gave them a sense of peace. Everyone on the board said it rang true to their own life. We're convinced this is the path we want to take for the future of our congregation."

"If that is the case, I would suggest we help each other."

"What do you mean?" Kendall asked.

"I will agree to help you and your congregation with a journey of discovery. We will discover how you are promoting healthy community now and how we can move forward in the future. In return, you will need to help me think through what would truly be helpful. Some of this may fail miserably. Are you game?"

"So," Kendall suggested, "you need a test lab?"

"That's right," I acknowledged. "I need someone who will help discover whether the ideas you found on the site will work in real life."

Kendall did not hesitate. "I'm game! I'll need to run this past my board, but I think they'll jump at the chance. How about I get back to you in a couple of days?" I could sense his excitement.

"That sounds great." I told him. "I will assemble a possible plan for the next step. We can review it in our next conversation."

Friday, 9:30 a.m.

When the phone rang, I knew before I picked it up that it was Kendall. "Joe, the board was excited about the opportunity to walk this journey with you. So where do we start? Have you come up with a first step?"

"I think I have a plan for the first step," I began. "I am very appreciative and excited that you are willing to be the lab. Please convey that to your leaders. Do you have e-mail?"

"Yes."

Kendall gave me his address and I sent him my rough thoughts as to the possibilities for step one.

Kendall,

I think the first step should be an evaluative step. We should try to answer these questions:

1. *What is the congregation's definition of belonging? What are the rules and regulations one needs to follow to belong? Are membership and belonging different?*
2. *What are the formal and informal groups that individuals can belong to in your congregation? Are there any rules or regulations for belonging to any of these?*

3. *How do we announce (or add support by talking about) the groups listed above? What words do we use to describe these groups? Do we, in any way, convey that belonging to one group is more valid than belonging to another group?*

4. *Tally the groups listed above into the four spaces on the Spatial Belonging Chart. Do we find harmony among the spaces? Are you surprised by what you have learned?*

5. *List your discoveries.*

Thanks again for your willingness to help. If you have any questions let me know.

Joe

Kendall received the e-mail while we were on the phone. "How does it look?" I asked.

"It looks to me like a great start. Can we go through a couple of the questions so I'm clear?" One thing about Kendall, he wasted no time. "First," he wondered, "who do you think I should invite to be on our first discovery team?"

"It may be best to limit this group at first," I suggested. "You could include the elder board and their spouses and maybe two leaders from your small group ministry. I would not get it too large."

Kendall asked, "How would you begin the first meeting? Should I start with the first question in your e-mail?"

That seemed a bit abrupt to me, so I said, "Maybe it would be best to bring those who have not been a part of the elder board's discussions up to date. From there you may want to help the discovery team grasp the essence of the questions by asking them to list the groups they belong to. Make sure to invite them to be as extensive as possible. For example, groups like television-viewing audience, home associations, sporting teams and sports played, groups within the church and outside. You get the idea."

Kendall interrupted, "Sure. That would help people get into the spirit of the idea. It probably would keep this from becoming a small group bashing session, too." He had another question. "What do you mean by the congregation's definition of belonging?"

"Every organization holds to a basic definition of what it means to belong: 'What must I do in order to belong to your congregation?' The answer comes from those who are already inside, those you consider to be members. What defines whether I am in or out? That's what we are trying to discover. It may be good to ask those who have recently 'joined' for their wisdom on the subject. These thoughts could be a good springboard for the discussion in the discovery team meeting."

"That's a great idea."

I had another thought. "If you get stuck, the two supporting questions about rules and membership should help."

Kendall said that he thought the second question would be easiest for the group and should be asked first, as it would relate directly to the list they prepared for their individual belongings. I agreed with him, and then he asked another question.

"Help me understand question number three. What do you mean by 'announcing' or 'supporting' the groups we're in? Do you mean that the way we talk about a group gives some indication of how important that group is?"

"Yes," I responded. "It is important to discover the language used to invite or uninvite someone into the groups you now have. To help this discussion along, you may want to collect past Sunday programs, announcement sheets, announcements put up on your screens and bulletin boards. Look at the tapes of past weekend services to listen to how groups were announced from the podium. You'll be able to see if you validate one group over another group—one kind of belonging over another kind."

Kendall interrupted, "Such as when we say, 'If you really want to experience what it means to belong here, you should attend a small group.'?"

"Exactly."

He said nothing for a moment but I could tell he was doing something. Then, "I've got your attachment up on my screen now: The Spatial Belonging Chart."

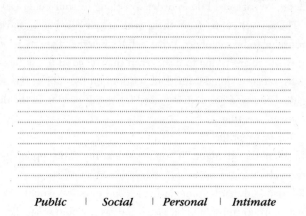

Public | *Social* | *Personal* | *Intimate*

"What do you think of it?" I wanted to know.

"I'm looking," he told me. "Am I to take the list of groups from question two and plot them on the chart?" Kendall asked.

"Yes. Remember to help the group by sharing the other attachment, The Four Spaces of Belonging Defined. That one explains each of the four spaces."

The Four Spaces of Belonging Defined

Public Space

Public belonging occurs when people connect through an outside influence. Fans of a sports team experience a sense of community because they cheer for the same team. They wear official garb, buy special broadcast viewing privileges, and stay up too late or get up extra early just to see the results of the game. These relationships carry great significance in our lives.

Social Space

Social belonging occurs when we share "snapshots" of what it would be like to be in personal space with us. The phrases "first impression" and "best foot forward" refer to this spatial belonging. You belong socially to your favorite bank teller, your pharmacist, or some of the people with whom you work.

Social belonging is important for two reasons. First, it provides the space for "neighbor" relationships. A neighbor is someone you know well enough to ask for (or provide) small favors. Second, it is important because it provides a safe "selection space or sorting space" for those with whom you would like to develop a "deeper" relationship. In social space we provide the information that helps others decide whether they connect with us. We get just enough information to decide to keep this person in this space or move them to another space.

Personal Space

Through personal belonging, we share private (not "naked") experiences, feelings, and thoughts. We call the people we connect to in this space "close friends." They are those who know more about us than an acquaintance would, yet not so much that they feel uncomfortable.

Intimate Space

In intimate belonging, we share "naked" experiences, feelings, and thoughts. We have very few relationships that are intimate. These people know the "naked truth" about us and the two of us are not "ashamed."

He said nothing as he continued to read. Then, "This is great. I think I've got it. I feel like I'm ready. I'll study what you've sent and get back with you if I have questions. I'll try to have our first meeting a week from tonight. Wish me luck."

Saturday, 7:00 p.m.

"Joe, this is Kendall." Surely he hadn't had his meeting already? Before I could ask, he explained.

"I'm calling to ask a couple of questions before our discovery team meeting tomorrow. Do you have a few minutes?" Kendall seemed rushed; it sounded as if he was calling from his car.

"Of course, what do you have for me?"

"Well I'm not trying to push, but do you have an idea of what step two will be? Usually at the close of each meeting we don't set another meeting unless we know why we'll be meeting. Several years ago we were having so many meetings it became toxic, so we put this into all our meeting agendas. It's really helped."

I had expected that I would need to supply the next step, but I was hoping it would come out of the first meeting. "Kendall," I asked, "can I think about it and e-mail you later tonight?"

Saturday, 11:00 p.m.

Kendall,

I hope your preparation for the meeting tomorrow afternoon has gone well. Here are some possible ideas for the next meeting agenda. We can talk over any questions you may have and explore other possibilities.

At the next meeting we could:

1. *Review the discoveries made at the first meeting.*
2. *Use the attached chart as a template to discover harmonious connections among the four spaces.*
3. *Choose one (maybe two) of the spaces where we can help individuals mature their experience of belonging.*
4. *Develop a plan for the space we choose.*

Call me if you have questions. I hope the meeting goes well.

Joe

Monday, 8:00 a.m.

"Joe! Kendall here. I hope I didn't wake you."

Kendall continued, "I wanted to call last night but it was late when I got home. The meeting was great. It's been a while since I've seen people come alive the way they did. As I talked everyone through the four spaces, you could almost see people loosen up. It was like a burden was lifted off their shoulders.

"One of the women—a huge supporter of small groups and one of the people we've been hearing from—said, 'I don't know if this is going to help this church, but it sure helps me understand my family better.'"

That was encouraging. "It sounds good," I told him. "I'm glad it helped."

"Helped?" Kendall was almost shouting. "It was like having flash-bulbs go off in people's heads. When people started listing all their 'belongings,' we even uncovered a couple of family secrets. You should have heard the laughter."

He paused. "There were those who didn't get it. Maybe they either couldn't see or weren't willing to put down all the groups or places they belonged to. When that happened, somebody would point out a place they had left out. Sometimes it was funny."

Kendall went on. "I don't think any of us realized how many different groups we belong to, especially after we started listing the informal ones. And the rules for belonging. Wow, did that cause discussion. People kept talking even when we broke for coffee. They talked about the spaces and how this one or that one related to their brother or their mother or someone at work. It was great."

I had a question: "Did you look at ways you announce your groups?"

"Yes," Kendall said. "I did it like a game: passed out paper and pencils, divided people into teams, and asked each team to look at our lists of groups and then write out announcements. First Church style. Like they were making Sunday morning announcements."

He was emphatic: "That was enlightening! I had sort of pre-pared myself, I guess, from reading your Web site and from the conversations I've had with you, so when the different groups read their announcements, I could see how we didn't talk about each group the same way; we didn't use the same words.

"I then asked them to list the groups in the order of importance based on how they wrote or heard the announcement. When I asked them to look at the words we use to describe, everybody could see the difference. Sometimes it was subtle, sometimes not. But the differences were there. Did we ever make one group more valid? Did we say one group was more important? Sure we did. People got uncomfortable."

Then I asked, "How long was this meeting? Were you able to finish all four questions?"

Kendall answered, "Before the meeting I had typed up the four spaces on a sheet of paper and made copies. I figured on using them when we got to the last question. But I could see a couple of people winding down, and I wanted to quit before people got tired. So I gave everybody the sheet of paper with the Four Spaces and asked them to sometime during the week fit each one of the groups on their lists into one of the four spaces. And if there was any connection between the spaces—you said 'harmony,' I think—to see if there was any 'harmony' and show that. Then bring these back to our next meeting. This gave us a good reason to have another meeting, and I think everybody wants to continue this. We're not ready to quit."

I asked Kendall, "Were there any surprises? What was the best secret you learned from the evening?"

Kendall laughed again. "The whole darn meeting was a surprise! But there is one idea I have for you. My wife suggested I get someone to take notes—someone who wouldn't participate—just take notes of things said, things written down, the little unspoken nuances and so on. I asked this lady from work. Her notes are priceless. She saw and heard things I would have missed."

"Like what?" I asked.

"I had no idea that we had four small groups that were afraid to tell anyone at the church that they were meeting for fear that we would mess it up," Kendall answered.

"Wow, that's really telling!"

"You bet it is," Kendall agreed. "We're getting together next Saturday for brunch and a meeting."

I was ready to wind this up for now. "Kendall," I told him, "you have shared some wonderful insight from your group. Can we talk midweek and go over the thoughts each of us will have as we head toward the next meeting?"

Thursday, 10:15 a.m.

Kendall,

I am sorry that I have not had a chance to call. I would like to see if there are any questions that I could discuss with you. I will be tied up until late tomorrow evening. So, it might be best for us to catch each other via e-mail.

Thanks for your willingness to contribute to this material.

Joe

Joe,

Thanks for checking in; I think all is well. I can't think of any questions, but I do have a story you might be interested in.

This has been a hectic week. I received a call Monday from the hospital saying I had a parishoner, Mrs. Kravetz, in ICU. I don't know a Mrs. Kravetz.

When I got to the hospital and to the ICU, she said my name and thanked me for coming. Long-story-short; she watches us every Sunday on TV. That's why she listed our church.

Kendall

Monday, 2:30 p.m.

"So, tell me," I asked, "how did the meeting go?" From the background noise, Kendall had called on his mobile phone.

"We had another great meeting," he said. "We plotted the groups we have in our church and compared that with the graph you sent showing harmony. By the way, why do you use 'harmony' instead of 'balance'?"

"Blame Leonard Sweet," I responded. "When I began this study, I used 'balance.' Then Leonard suggested that balance was not what I was describing. 'Balance' implies equal amounts. I am not promoting equal amounts of significant belonging in each of the four spaces.

What I am promoting is that health is found when we have a harmonious relationship among all four spatial connections."

"I can see that," Kendall affirmed.

Then I asked, "What did you discover as the group went through the plotting process?"

"I think we were surprised to find that we offer harmony right now with the different kinds of groups we have. What we don't do well is communicate that harmony. We need to reconsider how we advertise the groups, how we talk about them. We give some too much; we don't give other groups enough. In fact, we downplay most of these groups. So we may not need to adjust what we are offering; we just need to see how connections are created and how we communicate that."

"How did the discovery team feel about the finding?" I asked.

Kendall answered, "They seemed to be okay with what it indicated. Plus, I think everyone enjoyed the descriptive nature instead of this becoming one more thing for them to develop. It's always good to hear you're healthier than you thought."

I kept probing. "Were there any other discoveries? What else did the team find?"

"Well, they decided we should break up into smaller groups. Our group is too big to handle the next steps. Besides, if we go to smaller groups, we could bring in others from the congregation."

I was pleased that the group was not depending on me to develop the next steps.

Kendall continued, "We decided to concentrate on communication next, so we assigned four groups—a group for each of the spaces—to develop a plan to promote their specific space. By the way, I forgot to say it earlier, but Mrs. Kravetz is out of ICU. And you know what? She thinks she's part of our church."

"She may be," I told him. "Maybe not in the space you thought, but in a space that feels good to her."

"You're right."

"It sounds like things are going well," I told him, then asked, "How did the group respond?"

"Some wanted to wait and see if you had any ideas," Kendall explained, "but Marlene—she's a teacher and pretty sharp—said that we had a good handle on this and we should run with it. She said, 'If we run into a wall we know where to reach Joe.' Is that okay?"

"I think it's great! My hope was that this idea would be simple enough to employ and descriptive enough to understand quickly," I responded.

Kendall interrupted, "Oh, I almost forgot. At the end of our meeting, Frank suggested that we set up a group whose task would be to look at our physical space and how it communicates belonging and community. So we asked Frank if he would do this."

"Keep me informed on how things go," I requested. "I will help with anything you need. I will look forward to seeing how this helps you and the congregation."

Wednesday, 12:30 a.m.

Kendall,

I hope all is going well and you are finding that the language of the four spaces is helping. I have been thinking about your teams and their discoveries and I want to suggest a thought.

It may not be healthy to work on all four spaces at one time. It may help if you would pick one, maybe two, of the spaces and head toward health in those. Notice I said health. It would not be good to concentrate on one to the exclusion of the others. Nor would it be good to promote the one you choose as the most valid.

This is a thought you may want to wrestle with as the month comes to an end and you bring the team back together. Let me know what you think.

Joe

Friday, 6:00 p.m.

Joe,

I agree with your suggestion. Is there a space that you believe we should concentrate on first?

Our meeting is coming up next week. I have received very good comments from the team members I have talked with. Everyone is very excited about how this is going.

Kendall

Friday, 10:00 p.m.

Kendall,

Trust the wisdom of the group.

If I were making the decision in a vacuum I would start with social space. This is a space that our culture yearns to make significant connections in. Most of our culture tells us that these connections are not significant. If a congregation would promote this space as an important part of a person's search to belong and if the congregation would help individuals grow in this specific space, I believe you would find a lot of spillover health into the other spaces.

I hope this helps.

Joe

Monday, 10:00 a.m.

Joe,

I have attached some notes from our meeting. The notes are in bullet point and give an overview of what each team reported. Please look through these and let's talk on Wednesday. I think you are going to find these notes very interesting.

Thanks.

Kendall

Public Space

+ We promote worship as a "come as you are" public space.

+ We do not promote this space as a valid space to remain in— we instruct individuals to move closer or move on.

+ In worship we mix the spaces as we communicate the liturgy of the service (e.g., prayer is promoted as very personal/intimate). We are not sure personal prayer is appropriate in this public space.

+ We promoted a concert as public space.

Social Space

+ We have a lot of social spatial community in our congregation (e.g., the choir, the quilting club, the Boy Scouts). Yet we hardly ever announce these from the front on Sunday. In fact you almost have to "belong" here to find the secret places we hide these opportunities to connect.

+ When we do announce these kinds of social opportunities, we use them as "hooks" to get individuals to move closer to our congregation. Thus, we communicate that these are not valid places to remain.

Personal Space

+ We mention this term a lot. Especially as it relates to how we want individuals to relate to God.

+ We offer a lot of opportunities for this space in our small group ministry.

+ We promote this space as one of the spaces where you really belong.

+ We overemphasize this spatial belonging in our communication.

+ We believe that the 30 percent participation we now have in small groups may be the percentage that reflects health. 100 percent involvement is too much emphasis.

Intimate Space

+ We promote this space as the goal for every believer. This may be inappropriate.

+ We may be scaring individuals when we communicate that this is the goal.

+ We offer this space, but not at the degree that we promote it.

+ Some small groups report this kind of connection.

Wednesday, 2:00 p.m.

I started the conversation: "The insights from the team that you e-mailed are great! I think the group is well on its way to helping the congregation and individuals experience health in their search to belong. How did the team proceed from here?"

"We decided it was best to keep the small teams focused around the four spaces and then gather the teams from time to time to look at the big picture. Then we decided to focus on social space for the rest of the year, based on your suggestion." Kendall continued, "The one question everyone is hoping you could help us with is, 'What does it mean to help individuals grow in a specific space? And can you do this without moving them to another space?'"

I had expected this question earlier, but wanted to wait until he brought it up: "I believe you first have to help people recognize the connections they have in all four spaces and help them see the significance of each. Then you can help with specific spaces. It is not true that you have to process people from one space to another to help them grow. Each space has its specific competencies and disciplines. As I seek to help, I look at a person's learning style and then connect that style to the space."

"What do you mean by learning style?" he asked.

"I'm sending an e-mail with attachment that may help."

Learning Styles

+ Athletic
+ Intellectual
+ Extracurricular
+ Social
+ Fad of the moment
+ Outcast
+ Independent

Copyright © Kennon Callahan[2]

"There are several learning style models. I have found Callahan's to be most helpful. Suggest to your group that they think about how each of these learning styles uses the four spaces. For example, how do athletic learners use social space? Where do they find social space? What can they learn in social space and how? I would try to answer these questions for each learning style and each space."

"That helps," Kendall told me. Then he asked, "Is there a book where I could read about the learning styles?"

"Yes," I told him. "You can find them in Ken Callahan's book, *The Future That Has Come.* This is a helpful resource."

I continued, "The next issue may be to think through how to help individuals grow spiritual disciplines in each space. For example, it may help a social belonger to know how to pray in social space. This may not be out loud. But how does a person carry on an appropriate conversation with God in social space? How does a social belonger read the Bible? How does a social belonger serve? I believe in helping individuals grow in their walk with God in the space where they connect with him, and helping them use this as the means to move forward. I don't believe we must move them to another space for them to grow."

Kendall thought for a moment. Then, "That's great, Joe. It goes right along with one of the issues I have thought about. I believe there's been such a de-emphasis on public prayer in the last several years that we do not know how to present a good public prayer. Thus, we don't know how to teach public prayer—a public conversation with God."

"Good observation, Kendall," I told him. "Give me a minute to find it and I want to read you a paragraph from Neale Donald Walsch's book *Friendship with God: An Uncommon Dialogue.*

> Each of you experiences your conversations with God in your own way—and in different ways at different times. It will always be a two-way conversation, such as the one we are having right now. It could be a conversation "in your head," or on paper, or with My responses taking just a little more time, and reaching you in the form of the next song that you hear, or the next movie you see, or the next lecture you attend, or the next magazine article you read, or in the chance utterance of a friend whom you "just happen" to run into on the street.[3]

Then I went on, "In our push to move everyone into a personal or intimate relationship with God, we have forgotten the spectrum of ways God chooses to communicate with us—and the ways we choose to communicate with him. I believe that we are to help individuals with their connections with God in the space that they choose. We can help by providing opportunities for them to learn spiritual disciplines in that specific space."

"Let me see if I get this," Kendall began. "The next step is to teach people the significance of all of their connections. Then, try to develop environments that unite with their learning styles. And then show people how to develop spiritual disciplines in the specific space where they connect with God. Is that it?"

"This is a good start, Kendall. I think you and your congregation are on your way to discovering health and harmony in all four spaces."

How will you start your journey? What will you discover? Where do you belong? Who belongs to you?

Let me know who (and what) you find.

jmyers@languageofbelonging.com

+ *Bibliography*

Agre, Phil, ed. "Building Community Networks." *The Network Observer* 1, no. 12 (December 1994). http://dlis.gseis.ucla.edu/people/pagre/tno/december-1994.html

Alexander, Christopher, Murray Silverstein, Shlomo Angel, Sara Ishikawa, and Denny Abrams. *The Oregon Experiment*. New York: Oxford University Press, 1975.

Alexander, Christopher, Sara Ishikawa, and Murray Silverstein, with Max Jacobson, Ingrid Fiksdahl-King, and Shlomo Angel. *A Pattern Language: Towns • Buildings • Construction*. New York: Oxford University Press, 1977.

Alexander, Christopher. *The Timeless Way of Building*. New York: Oxford University Press, 1979.

Apsel, Joyce. "Belonging and Being an Outsider: Chapter 12." *St. Petersburg Times* (November 29, 1999). http://sptimes.com/News/112999/NIE/Belonging_and_being_a.shtml

Armour, Michael C. and Don Browning. *Systems-Sensitive Leadership*. Joplin, Mo.: College Press, 2000.

Armstrong, David. *Managing by Storying Around: A New Method of Leadership*. New York: Doubleday/Currency, 1992.

Armstrong, Karen. *The Battle for God*. New York: Ballantine Books, 2000.

Arnold, Eberhard. *Why We Live in Community*. 3rd English ed. Farmington, Pa.: Plough Publishing House, 1995.

Asher, Mark. *Body Language: Easy Ways to Get the Most from Your Relationships, Work and Love Life*. New York: Barnes & Noble Books, 2002.

"Assessment and Evolution of Community Networking." (Presented at the "Ties That Bind" Conference on Building Community Computing Networks sponsored by Apple Computer and the Morino Institute, Cupertino, Calif., May 5, 1994). http://morino.org/assessment.htm#assessment

Avis, Andrew. "Public Spaces on the Information Highway: The Role of Community Networks." Master's thesis, University of Calgary, 1995. http://www.ucalgary.ca/UofC/faculties/GNST/theses/avis/thesis.html

Axelrod, Alan. *Elizabeth I CEO: Strategic Lessons from the Leader Who Built an Empire*. Paramus, N.J.: Prentice Hall Press, 2000.

Bailey, Beth L. *From Front Porch to Back Seat: Courtship in Twentieth-Century America*. Baltimore: The Johns Hopkins University Press, 1988, 1989.

Baker, Mark C. *The Atoms of Language: The Mind's Hidden Rules of Grammar*. New York: Basic Books, 2001.

Barabási, Albert-László. *Linked: The New Science of Networks*. Cambridge, Mass.: Perseus Publishing, 2002.

Bass, Diana Butler. *Strength for the Journey: A Pilgrimage of Faith in Community*. San Francisco: Jossey-Bass, 2002.

Baugh, Ken, and Rich Hurst. *Getting Real: An Interactive Guide to Relational Ministry*. Colorado Springs: NavPress, 2000.

Bellah, Robert N., Richard Madsen, William M. Sullivan, Ann Swidler, and Steven Tipton. *Habits of the Heart: Individualism and Commitment in American Life*. Berkeley: University of California Press, 1985, 1996.

Berry, Wendell. *The Unsettling of America: Culture & Agriculture*, San Francisco: Sierra Club Books, 1977.

Bilezikian, Gilbert. *Community 101: Reclaiming the Local Church as Community of Oneness*. Grand Rapids: Zondervan, 1997.

Bohl, Charles C. *Place Making: Developing Town Centers, Main Streets, and Urban Villages*. Washington, D.C.: ULI—the Urban Land Institute, 2002.

Bond, Meg A. "Gender, Race, and Class in Organizational Contexts." *American Journal of Community Psychology* 27, no. 3 (1999): 327–354. Abstract. http://www.pressroom.com/~afrimale/bond.htm

Bonhoeffer, Dietrich. *Life Together: A Discussion of Christian Fellowship*. San Francisco: HarperCollins, 1954.

Boothman, Nicholas. *How to Make People Like You in 90 Seconds or Less*. New York: Workman Publishing, 2000.

Brand, Paul, and Philip Yancey. *In His Image*. Grand Rapids: Zondervan, 1984.

Bridges, Jerry. *The Discipline of Grace: God's Role and Our Role in the Pursuit of Holiness*. Colorado Springs: NavPress, 1994.

Brooks, David. *Bobos in Paradise: Bourgeois Bohemians: The New Upper Class and How They Got There*. New York: Simon & Schuster, 2000.

Brooks, Michael. *Instant Rapport: Instant Charisma. . . Instant Chemistry. . . Instant Intimacy*. New York: Warner Books, 1989.

Buber, Martin. *I and Thou*. Translation by Walter Kaufmann. New York: Charles Scribner's Sons, 1970.

Buchanan, Mark. *Nexus: Small Worlds and the Groundbreaking Science of Networks*. New York: W. W. Norton, 2002.

Callahan, Kennon L. *Effective Church Leadership: Building on the Twelve Keys*. San Francisco: HarperCollins, 1990.

Callahan, Kennon L. *The Future That Has Come: New Possibilities for Reaching and Growing the Grass Roots*. San Francisco: Jossey-Bass, 2002.

Callahan, Kennon L. *Small, Strong Congregations: Creating Strengths and Health for Your Congregation*. San Francisco: Jossey-Bass, 2000.

Callahan, Kennon L. *Twelve Keys to an Effective Church: The Leaders' Guide*. San Francisco: Harper & Row, 1987.

Carson, D.A., ed. *Telling the Truth: Evangelizing Postmoderns*. Grand Rapids: Zondervan, 2000.

Chester, Laura. *Holy Personal: Looking for Small Private Places of Worship*. Bloomington: Indiana University Press, 2000.

Clores, Suzanne. *Memoirs of a Spiritual Outsider*. Berkeley: Conari Press, 2000.

Cloud, Henry, and John Townsend. *How People Grow: What the Bible Reveals about Personal Growth*. Grand Rapids: Zondervan, 2001.

College Hill Presbyterian Church. "What Gives You a Sense of Belonging?" *Bell Tower News* 50, no. 1 (January–February 2001).

Conyers, A.J. "Why the Chattahoochee Sings: Notes Towards a Theory of 'Place'." *Modern Age—A Quarterly Review* 43, no. 2 (Spring 2001).

Corbin, Carolyn. *Great Leaders See the Future First: Taking Your Organization to the Top in Five Revolutionary Steps*. Chicago: Dearborn, 2000.

Crabb, Larry. *Connecting: Healing for Ourselves and Our Relationships—A Radical New Vision*. Nashville: Word, 1997.

Crabtree, Andy. "Remarks on the Social Organization of Space and Place." *Journal of Mundane Behavior* 1, no. 1 (February 2000). http://www.mundanebehavior.org/issues/v1n1/crabtree.htm

Craddock, Fred B. *Overhearing the Gospel: Preaching and Teaching the Faith to Persons Who Have Heard It All Before*. Nashville: Abingdon, 1978.

Davenport, Thomas H., and John C. Beck. *The Attention Economy: Understanding the New Currency of Business*. Boston: Harvard Business School Press, 2001.

"The Delirious Delirium." *Worship Leader* 10, no. 5 (July/August, 2001).

DeVito, Joseph A. *Messages: Building Interpersonal Communication Skills*, 4th ed. New York: Longman, 1999.

Devlin, Rebekah. "A Mother's Search for Belonging." *The Age* (May 26, 2000). http://www.theage.com.au

Duany, Andres, Elizabeth Plater-Zyberk, and Jeff Speck. *Suburban Nation: The Rise of Sprawl and the Decline of the American Dream*. New York: North Point Press, 2000.

Dyrness, William A. *Visual Faith: Art, Theology, and Worship in Dialogue*. Grand Rapids: Baker Academic, 2001.

Ellin, Nan. *Postmodern Urbanism*. New York: Princeton Architectural Press, 1996.

Erickson, Millard J. *Postmodernizing the Faith: Evangelical Responses to the Challenge of Postmodernism*. Grand Rapids: Baker Books, 1998.

Etuk, Emma Samuel. *Friends: What Would I Do Without Them? Finding Real and Valuable Friendships in an Unfriendly World*. Washington, D.C.: Emida International Publishers, 1999.

Etzioni, A. *The Spirit of Community*. New York: Crown, 1993.

Farson, Richard. *Management of the Absurd: Paradoxes in Leadership*. New York: Simon & Schuster, 1996.

Field, Taylor, and Jo Kadlecek. *A Church Called Graffiti: Finding Grace on the Lower East Side*. Nashville: Broadman & Holman, 2001.

Flinders, Carol Lee. *The Values of Belonging: Rediscovering Balance, Mutuality, Intuition, and Wholeness in a Competitive World*. New York: HarperCollins, 2002.

Florida, Richard. *The Rise of the Creative Class and How It's Transforming Work, Leisure, Community and Everyday Life*. New York: Basic Books, 2002.

Ford, Larry R. *The Spaces between Buildings*. Baltimore: The Johns Hopkins University Press, 2000.

Frazee, Randy. *The Connecting Church: Beyond Small Groups to Authentic Community*. Grand Rapids: Zondervan, 2001.

Garner, Alan. *Conversationally Speaking*. New York: McGraw-Hill, 1980, 1981, 1988.

Gibbs, Eddie. *Church Next: Quantum Changes in How We Do Ministry*. Downers Grove, Ill.: InterVarsity Press, 2000.

Gladwell, Malcolm. *The Tipping Point: How Little Things Can Make a Big Difference*. Boston: Little, Brown and Company, 2000, 2002.

Graham, Garth. "A Domain Where Thought Is Free to Roam: The Social Purpose of Community Networks." A background paper supporting Telecommunities Canada's appearance, March 29, 1995, at the CRTC public hearings on information highway convergence (March 29, 1995). http://www.tc.ca/crtc.brief.html

"Green Space Fosters Social Ties, Study Finds." *Environmental News Network* (May 10, 1999). http://www.enn.com/enn-news-archive/1999/05/0510/99/greenspace_3096.asp

Gruchow, Paul. *Grass Roots: The Universe of Home*. Minneapolis: Milkweed Editions, 1995.

Guder, Darrell L. *Missional Church: A Vision for the Sending of the Church in North America*. Grand Rapids: Eerdmans, 1998.

Haggard, Ted. *Dog Training, Fly Fishing, & Sharing Christ in the 21st Century: Empowering Your Church to Build Community Through Shared Interests*. Nashville: Thomas Nelson, 2002.

Hall, Edward T. *Beyond Culture*. New York: Anchor Books/Doubleday, 1976, 1981.

Hall, Edward T. *The Hidden Dimension*. New York: Anchor Books/Doubleday, 1966, 1982.

Hall, Edward T. *The Silent Language*. New York: Anchor Books, 1959, 1981.

Hendricks, William D. *Exit Interviews: Revealing Stories of Why People Are Leaving the Church*. Chicago: Moody Press, 1993.

Henry, Patrick. *The Ironic Christian's Companion: Finding the Marks of God's Grace in the World*. New York: Riverhead Books, 1999.

Hesselbein, Frances, Marshall Goldsmith, Richard Beckhard, and Richard F. Schubert, eds. *The Drucker Foundation: The Community of the Future*. San Francisco: Jossey-Bass, 1998.

Heyduck, Richard. *The Recovery of Doctrine in the Contemporary Church: An Essay in Philosophical Ecclesiology*. Waco, Tex.: Baylor University Press, 2002.

Horrocks, Christopher. *Postmodern Encounters: Marshall McLuhan and Virtuality*. Cambridge, U.K.: Icon Books, 2000.

Hunt, Morton. *The Story of Psychology*. New York: Anchor/Doubleday, 1993.

Hunter, A. "The Loss of Community: An Empirical Test Through Replication." *American Sociological Review* 40, 537–552, 1975.

Hunter, George G., III. *The Celtic Way of Evangelism: How Christianity Can Reach the West . . . Again*. Nashville: Abingdon, 2000.

Hunter, George G., III. *Church for the Unchurched*. Nashville: Abingdon, 1996.

Ignatieff, Michael. *The Needs of Strangers*. New York: Picador USA, 1984.

Jakobovits, Leon A. "Graphic Concepts as a Listening and Thinking Tool—A Demonstration." Colloquium memorandum (October 30, 1981). http://www.soc.hawaii.edu/leonj/499s98/travisa/138-140.htm

Jameson, Fredric. *The Cultural Turn: Selected Writings on the Postmodern, 1983–1998*. London: Verso, 1998.

Johnson, Steven. *Emergence: The Connected Lives of Ants, Brains, Cities, and Software*. New York: Scribner, 2001.

Johnston, John. "They Like to Sit a Spell for Bingo." *Cincinnati Enquirer* (Tuesday, January 29, 2002): C-1.

Jones, Tony. *Postmodern Youth Ministry: Exploring Cultural Shift, Cultivating Authentic Community, Creating Holistic Connections*. Grand Rapids: Zondervan/Youth Specialties, 2001.

Kallenberg, Brad J. *Live to Tell: Evangelism for a Postmodern Age*. Grand Rapids: Brazos Press, 2002.

Karlen, Arno. *Biography of a Germ*. New York: Anchor Books, 2000.

Keel, Philipp. *All About Me*. New York: Broadway Books, 1998.

Kegan, Robert, and Lisa Laskow Lahey. *How the Way We Talk Can Change the Way We Work: Seven Languages for Transformation*. San Francisco: Jossey-Bass, 2001.

Keillor, Garrison. *Lake Wobegon Summer 1956*. New York: Viking, 2001.

Kelly, Gerard. *RetroFuture: Rediscovering Our Roots, Recharting Our Routes*. Downers Grove, Ill: InterVarsity Press, 1999.

Ketcherside, W. Carl, ed. "About the Church." *Mission Messenger* 35, no. 3 (March 1973).

Kissel, Adam, and Valerie Photos. "Discussing an Intimate Question with Ten Thousand of Your Closest Friends: You Gonna Do That in Public?" *re:generation Quarterly* 7, no. 3 (Fall 2001).

Kop, Yaakov, and Robert E. Litan. *Sticking Together: The Israeli Experiment in Pluralism.* Washington, D.C.: Brookings Institution Press, 2002.

Kreiser, Klaus, team leader. "Forms of Belonging and Modes of Social Integration." Research program on Individual and Society in the Mediterranean Muslim World. Themes issued from the European Science Foundation Granada Plenary Conference (May 24–27, 1996). http://www.hf.uib.no/smi/eurames/ismm1.html

Kretzmann, John P., and John L. McKnight. *Building Communities from the Inside Out: A Path Toward Finding and Mobilizing a Community's Assets.* Evanston, Ill.: The Asset-Based Community Development Institute, Institute for Policy Research, Northwestern University, 1993.

Kronberg, Matt, Mike Peterson, Jedd Medefind, and Trey Sklar. *Four Souls.* Nashville: W Publishing Group, 2001.

Lawson, LeRoy. *The Family of God: The Meaning of Church Membership.* Cincinnati: Standard Publishing, 1980.

Lesser, Elizabeth. *The New American Spirituality: A Seeker's Guide.* New York: Random House, 1999.

Lewis, Robert. *The Church of Irresistible Influence.* Grand Rapids: Zondervan, 2001.

Lingis, Alphonso. *The Community of Those Who Have Nothing in Common.* Bloomington: Indiana University Press, 1994.

Locke, John L. *Why We Don't Talk to Each Other Anymore: The De-Voicing of Society.* New York: Touchstone, 1998.

Lovell, Nadia, ed. *Locality and Belonging.* London: Routledge, 1998.

Lyotard, Jean-François. *The Postmodern Condition: A Report on Knowledge.* Translation from the French by Geoff Bennington and Brian Massumi. Minneapolis: University of Minnesota Press, 1979, 1984.

Lyotard, Jean-François. *The Postmodern Explained: Correspondence 1982–1985.* Translation edited by Julian Pefanis and Morgan Thomas. Minneapolis: University of Minnesota Press, 1988, 1992.

Manning, Brennan. *The Signature of Jesus.* Sisters, Ore.: Multnomah, 1988, 1992, 1996.

Mason, Andrew. *Community, Solidarity and Belonging: Levels of Community and Their Normative Significance.* Cambridge, U.K.: Cambridge University Press, 2000.

Mattessich, Paul, Barbara Monsey, and Corinna Roy. *Community Building: What Makes It Work: A Review of Factors Influencing Successful Community Building.* St. Paul, Minn.: Amherst H. Wilder Foundation, 1997.

McGee, Robert S. *The Search for Significance*. Houston: Rapha, 1985, 1990.

McGraw, Phillip C. *Self Matters: Creating Your Life from the Inside Out*. New York: Simon & Schuster Source, 2001.

McGregor, Douglas. *The Human Side of Enterprise*. New York: McGraw-Hill, 1960, 1985.

McKenna, Patrick, and David H. Maister. *First Among Equals: How to Manage a Group of Professionals*. New York: The Free Press, 2002.

McKnight, John. *The Careless Society: Community and Its Counterfeits*. New York: Basic Books, 1995.

McLaren, Brian D. *The Church on the Other Side: Doing Ministry in the Postmodern Matrix*. Grand Rapids: Zondervan, 1998, 2000.

McLaren, Brian D. *More Ready Than You Realize: Evangelism as Dance in the Postmodern Matrix*. Grand Rapids: Zondervan, 2002.

McLaren, Brian D. *A New Kind of Christian*. San Francisco: Jossey-Bass, 2001.

McManus, Erwin Raphael. *An Unstoppable Force: Daring to Become the Church God Had in Mind*. Loveland, Col.: Group, 2001.

McMillan, D.W., and Chavis, D.M. "Sense of Community: A Definition and Theory." *Journal of Community Psychology* 14, 6–23, 1986.

Meadows, Susannah. "Meet the Gamma Girls," *Newsweek*, June 3, 2002.

Middelton-Moz, Jane, and Mary Lee Zawadski. *Bullies: From the Playground to the Boardroom: Strategies for Survival*. Deerfield Beach, Fla.: Health Communications, Inc., 2002.

Morgenthaler, Sally. *Worship Evangelism: Inviting Unbelievers into the Presence of God*. Grand Rapids: Zondervan, 1995.

Moser-Wellman, Annette. *The Five Faces of Genius: The Skills to Master Ideas at Work*. New York: Viking, 2001.

Murphy, Nancey. *Beyond Liberalism & Fundamentalism: How Modern and Postmodern Philosophy Set the Theological Agenda*. Harrisburg, Pa.: Trinity Press International, 1996.

Murunga, Godwin R. "Creating a Sense of Belonging in the City of Nairobi through Participatory Governance." University of Toronto Centre for Urban and Community Studies Presentation (November 26, 1999). Seminar description. http://www.utoronto.ca/env/seminars/cucs.htm

Myers, William R. *Becoming and Belonging: A Practical Design for Confirmation*. Book synopsis. http://www.ucpress.com/books/book-0942-2.html

Nasar, J.L., and D.A. Julian. "The Psychological Sense of Community in the Neighborhood. *Journal of the American Planning Association* 61 (1995): 178–184.

Nisbet, R. *The Quest for Community*. New York: Oxford University Press, 1953.

Norris, Kathleen. *Amazing Grace: A Vocabulary of Faith*. New York: Riverhead Books, 1998.

Norris, Kathleen. *Dakota: A Spiritual Geography*. New York: Houghton Mifflin, 1993, 2001.

Norris, Kathleen. *The Virgin of Bennington*. New York: Riverhead Books, 2001.

O'Brien, Jodi, and Peter Kollock. *The Production of Reality: Essays and Readings on Social Interaction*, 3rd ed. Thousand Oaks, Calif.: Pine Forge Press, 2001.

Oldenburg, Ray, ed. *Celebrating the Third Place: Inspiring Stories About the "Great Good Places" at the Heart of Our Communities*. New York: Marlowe & Company, 2001.

Oldenburg, Ray. *The Great Good Place: Cafés, Coffee Shops, Bookstores, Bars, Hair Salons and Other Hangouts at the Heart of a Community*. New York: Marlowe & Company, 1989, 1997, 1999.

Olson, Traci. "Analysis of Cultural Communication and Proxemics." http://www.unl.edu/casetudy/456/traci.htm

Olsson, Karl A. *Meet Me on the Patio: New Relational Bible Studies for Individuals and Groups*. Minneapolis: Augsburg, 1977.

Pargament, Kenneth I. *The Psychology of Religion and Coping: Theory, Research, Practice*. New York: The Guilford Press, 1997.

Pascale, Richard T., Mark Millemann, and Linda Gioja. *Surfing the Edge of Chaos: The Laws and Nature and the New Laws of Business*. New York: Crown Business, 2000.

Paul, Pamela. *The Starter Marriage and the Future of Matrimony*. New York: Random House, 2002.

Perin, Constance. *Belonging in America: Reading Between the Lines*. Madison: The University of Wisconsin Press, 1988.

Petersen, Jim. *Church Without Walls: Moving Beyond Traditional Boundaries*. Colorado Springs: NavPress, 1992.

Poe, Edgar Allan. *The Complete Tales and Poems of Edgar Allan Poe*. New York: The Modern Library, 1938.

Popcorn, Faith, and Adam Hanft. *Dictionary of the Future: The Words, Terms, and Trends that Define the Way We'll Live, Work and Talk*. New York: Hyperion, 2001.

Powers, John S. *Redefining Church Membership: From Myth to Ministry*. Nashville: Lifeway, 2001.

Putnam, Robert D. *Bowling Alone: The Collapse and Revival of American Community*. New York: Simon & Schuster, 2000.

"The Quality of Life Profile: A Generic Measure of Health and Well-Being." http://www.utoronto.ca/qol/profile.htm

Reich, Robert B. *The Future of Success*. New York: Alfred A. Knopf, 2000.

Rheingold, Howard. *Smart Mobs: The Next Social Revolution*. Cambridge, Mass.: Perseus Publishing, 2002.

Riddell, Michael. *Threshold of the Future: Reforming the Church in the Post-Christian West*. London: Society for Promoting Christian Knowledge, 1998.

Robinson, Dave. *Postmodern Encounters: Nietzsche and Postmodernism*. Cambridge, U.K.: Icon Books, 1999.

Rohr, Richard. *Hope Against Darkness: The Transforming Vision of Saint Francis in an Age of Anxiety*. Cincinnati: St. Anthony Messenger Press, 2001.

Rosen, Emanuel. *The Anatomy of Buzz: How to Create Word of Mouth Marketing*. New York: Doubleday/Currency, 2000.

Rosenau, Pauline Marie. *Post-Modernism and the Social Sciences: Insights, Inroads, and Intrusions*. Princeton, N.J.: Princeton University Press, 1992.

Rybczynski, Witold. *Looking Around: A Journey Through Architecture*. New York: Penguin, 1992.

Sanders, T. Irene. *Strategic Thinking and the New Science: Planning in the Midst of Chaos, Complexity, and Change*. New York: The Free Press, 1998.

Schaef, Anne Wilson. *Escape from Intimacy: The Pseudo-Relationship Addictions*. New York: HarperCollins, 1989.

Schuler, Doug. "Creating Public Space in Cyberspace: The Rise of the New Community Networks." *Internet World* (December 1995). (This version differs slightly from the printed version.) http://www.vcn.bc.ca/sig/comm-nets/schuler.html

Searle, John R. *Mind, Language and Society: Philosophy in the Real World*. New York: Basic Books, 1998.

Simmons, Rachel. *Odd Girl Out: The Hidden Culture of Aggression in Girls*. New York: Harcourt, 2002.

Sjogren, Steve. *101 Ways to Reach Your Community*. Colorado Springs: NavPress, 2001.

Smith, Anna Deavere. *Talk to Me: Listening Between the Lines*. New York: Random House, 2000.

Smith, Chuck, jr. *The End of the World . . . As We Know It: Clear Direction for Bold and Innovative Ministry in a Postmodern World*. Colorado Springs: Waterbrook Press, 2001.

Smith, James Bryan. *Rich Mullins: His Life and Legacy—An Arrow Pointing to Heaven*. Nashville: Broadman & Holman, 2000.

Snyder, Howard A. *The Community of the King*. Downers Grove, Ill.: Inter-Varsity Press, 1977.

Soja, Edward W. *Postmodern Geographies: The Reassertion of Space in Critical Social Theory*. London: Verso, 1989.

Spong, John Shelby. *A New Christianity for a New World: Why Traditional Faith Is Dying & How a New Faith Is Being Born*. San Francisco: HarperCollins, 2001.

Stanley, Paul D., and J. Robert Clinton. *Connecting: The Mentoring Relationships You Need to Succeed in Life*. Colorado Springs: NavPress, 1992.

Stein, Arlene. *The Stranger Next Door: The Story of a Small Community's Battle over Sex, Faith, and Civil Rights*. Boston: Beacon Press, 2001.

Susanka, Sarah. *Creating the Not So Big House: Insights and Ideas for the New American Home*. Newtown, Conn.: Taunton Press, 2001.

Sweet, Leonard. *Aqua Church*. Loveland, Col.: Group, 1999.

Sweet, Leonard. *Carpe Mañana: Is Your Church Ready to Seize Tomorrow?* Grand Rapids: Zondervan, 2001.

Sweet, Leonard. *Post-Modern Pilgrims: First Century Passion for the 21st Century World*. Nashville: Broadman & Holman, 2000.

Tapscott, Don. *Growing Up Digital: The Rise of the Net Generation*. New York: McGraw-Hill, 1998.

Tarlow, Mikela, and Philip Tarlow. *Digital Aboriginal: The Direction of Business Now: Instinctive, Nomadic, and Ever-Changing*. New York: Warner Books, 2002.

Taylor, Mark C. *The Moment of Complexity: Emerging Network Culture*. Chicago: The University of Chicago Press, 2001.

Tidwell, Jenifer. "Common Ground: A Pattern Language for Human-Computer Interface Design." (May 17, 1999). http://www.mit.edu/~jtidwell/common_ground_onefile.html

Towns, Elmer, and Warren Bird. *Into the Future: Turning Today's Church Trends into Tomorrow's Opportunities*. Grand Rapids: Fleming H. Revell, 2000.

Trueblood, Elton. *The Company of the Committed*. New York: Harper & Row, 1961.

Unger, D., and A. Wandersman. "The Importance of Neighbors: The Social, Cognitive, and Affective Components of Neighboring." *American Journal of Community Psychology* 13 (1985): 139–169.

Visser, Margaret. *The Geometry of Love: Space, Time, Mystery, and Meaning in an Ordinary Church*. New York: North Point Press, 2000.

Wallerstein, Immanuel. *The End of the World As We Know It: Social Science for the Twenty-First Century*. Minneapolis: University of Minnesota Press, 1999.

Walsch, Neale Donald. *Friendship with God: An Uncommon Dialogue*. New York: G. P. Putnam's Sons, 1999.

Weber, Larry. *The Provocateur: How a New Generation of Leaders Are Building Communities, Not Just Companies*. New York: Crown Business, 2001.

Weinberger, David. *Small Pieces Loosely Joined: A Unified Theory of the Web*. Cambridge, Mass.: Perseus Publishing, 2002.

Wenger, Etienne, Richard McDermott, and William M. Snyder. *Cultivating Communities of Practice: A Guide to Managing Knowledge*. Boston: Harvard Business School Press, 2002.

Whitehead, Barbara Dafoe. *The Divorce Culture*. New York: Alfred A. Knopf, 1997.

Willard, Dallas. *The Divine Conspiracy: Rediscovering Our Hidden Life in God*. San Francisco: HarperCollins, 1998.

Willard, Dallas. *In Search of Guidance: Developing a Conversational Relationship with God*. New York: HarperCollins, 1993.

Williams, Leslie. *Night Wrestling: Struggling for Answers and Finding God*. Dallas: Word, 1997.

Wilson, Jon. "A Sense of Belonging." *Hope Magazine* (January/February 1997). http://www.hopemag.com/Pages/Jon_editorials_pages/6.htm

Wolfram, Stephen. *A New Kind of Science*. Champaign, Ill.: Wolfram Media, Inc., 2002.

Yancey, Philip. *Soul Survivor: How My Faith Survived the Church*. New York: Doubleday, 2001.

Zander, Rosamund Stone, and Benjamin Zander. *The Art of Possibility: Transforming Professional and Personal Life*. Boston: Harvard Business School Press, 2000.

+ *End Notes*

+ Chapter 1: The Myths of Belonging

1. Rem Koolhaas, in a guest editorial for a special issue of *Wired*. This issue presents an "atlas" that catalogs "emerging spaces" and "the seeds of the coming culture." *Wired* (June 2003), 117.

2. Condensed from "The Accidental Honeymoon OA," http://off-the-map.org/oa/restaurant_oas.html, retrieved April 28, 2003. "OA" stands for "Ordinary Attempts," people's ordinary attempts to have significant conversations about spiritual things. Jim Henderson, the group's founder, describes evangelism this way: Ordinary things ordinary people ordinarily do.

3. Kennon L. Callahan, *Effective Church Leadership: Building on the Twelve Keys* (San Francisco: Harper & Row, 1990), 106. [*Effective Church Leadership: Building on the Twelve Keys*, Kennon L. Callahan, copyright 1990 by Kennon L. Callahan. Reprinted by permission of John Wiley and Sons, Inc.]

4. George Bullard, "Abandon Committees, Skip Teams and Embrace Communities," *Explorer*, no. 66 (December 5, 2002), http://www.leadnet.org/allthingsln/archive_template.asp?archive_id=86&db=explorer, retrieved April 28, 2003.

5. Randy Frazee, *The Connecting Church: Beyond Small Groups to Authentic Community* (Grand Rapids: Zondervan, 2001), 132.

6. Ignatieff, *The Needs of Strangers* (New York: Picador USA, 1984), 141.

7. Edward T. Hall, *The Hidden Dimension* (New York: Anchor Books/Doubleday, 1966, 1982), 94.

8. Larry Crabb in the foreword of Frazee, *The Connecting Church*, 13.

9. Hall, *The Hidden Dimension*, 1.

10. Ibid., 117–124.

11. Frazee, *The Connecting Church*, 35.

+ Chapter 2: Longing to Belong

1.   George Gallup Jr., *The People's Religion* (New York: Macmillan, 1989), quoted in Randy Frazee, *The Connecting Church: Beyond Small Groups to Authentic Community* (Grand Rapids: Zondervan, 2001), 24.

2.   Mary Moore, quoted in "In Search of Belonging: The Hispanic Religious Presence in Indianapolis," *Religion & Community* 4, no. 1 (Fall 1998), http://www.polis.iupui.edu/RUC/Newsletters/Religion/vol 4no1.htm, retrieved April 28, 2003.

3.   Luke 15:11–32.

4.   From a speech given by Lyle Schaller at a Leadership Network Conference in Ontario, California, October 1998, quoted in Frazee, *The Connecting Church*, 37.

5.   Rose Swetman, "First They Fast—Then They Follow," *Off the Map Update*, December 2001 (e-newsletter). [Used by permission of www.off-the-map.org.]

6.   Kathleen Norris, *Amazing Grace: A Vocabulary of Faith* (New York: Riverhead Books, 1998), 5–7.

7.   Michael Ignatieff, *The Needs of Strangers* (New York: Picador USA, 1984), 139.

8.   Quoted in Stephen Neill, *A History of Christian Missions* (Baltimore: Penguin, 1964), 42.

9.   Luke 10:25–29.

10.   Leonard Sweet, "The Quest for Community," *Leadership Journal* XX, no. 4 (Fall 1999), 33.

11.   Elton Trueblood, *The Company of the Committed* (New York: Harper & Row, 1961), 9.

12.   Francis Schaeffer, quoted in Frazee, *The Connecting Church*, 85.

13.   Matthew 25:38.

+ **Chapter 3: "Give Me Some Space"**

1. The Doors, "People Are Strange," *Strange Days*,
    Elektra/Asylum Records, October 1967, vinyl.

2. Edward T. Hall, *The Hidden Dimension* (New York: Anchor
    Books/Doubleday, 1966, 1982), 117–124.

3. Ibid., 1.

4. Alan Garner, *Conversationally Speaking* (New York: McGraw-
    Hill, 1988), 132–133.

5. Howard Rheingold, *Smart Mobs: The Next Social Revolution*
    (Cambridge, Mass.: Perseus Publishing, 2002), 167.

6. John Johnston, "They Like to Sit a Spell for Bingo," *Cincinnati
    Enquirer*, Tuesday, January 29, 2002, C-1.

7. Jennifer Krause, "The Ones Who Turn Up Along the Way,"
    Newsweek (November 26, 2001), 14–15.

8. Michael Suk-Young Chwe, *Rational Ritual: Culture, Coordination,
    and Common Knowledge* (Princeton: Princeton University Press,
    2001), http://www.chwe.net/michael/r.pdf (6 March 2002),
    quoted in Howard Rheingold, *Smart Mobs*, 176.

9. Matthew 8:5–13.

10. John L. Locke, *Why We Don't Talk to Each Other Anymore: The De-
    Voicing of Society* (New York: Touchstone, 1998), 61.

11. Philip Blumstein, "The Production of Selves in Personal
    Relationships," in *The Production of Reality: Essays and Readings on
    Social Interaction*, 3rd ed. by Jodi O'Brien and Peter Kollock
    (Thousand Oaks, Calif.: Pine Forge Press, 2001), 299.

12. Robert D. Putnam, *Bowling Alone: The Collapse and Revival of
    American Community* (New York: Simon & Schuster, 2000),
    18–19, quoting Doug McAdam, *Freedom Summer* (New York:
    Oxford University Press, 1988), 14–15; James Q. Wilson,
    "Why Are We Having a Wave of Violence?" *The New York Times
    Magazine* (May 19, 1968), 120; and Lyda Judson Hanifan, "The
    Rural School Community Center," *Annals of the American
    Academy of Political and Social Science* 67 (1916): 130–138, quo-
    tation at 130.

13. Larry Crabb, *Connecting: Healing for Ourselves and Our Relationships: A Radical New Vision* (Nashville: Word Publishing, 1997), xi.

14. See Genesis 2:25–3:10.

15. Joan P. Emerson, "Behavior in Private Places: Sustaining Definitions of Reality in Gynecological Examinations," in O'Brien and Kollock, *The Production of Reality*, 267.

16. Kennon L. Callahan, *Effective Church Leadership: Building on the Twelve Keys* (San Francisco: Harper, 1990), 102. [*Effective Church Leadership: Building on the Twelve Keys*, Kennon L. Callahan, copyright 1990 by Kennon L. Callahan. Reprinted by permission of John Wiley and Sons, Inc.]

17. Crabb, *Connecting*, xiii.

+ Chapter 4: Group Chemistry

1. Mark Buchanan, *Nexus: Small Worlds and the Groundbreaking Science of Networks* (New York: W. W. Norton & Company, 2002), 15.

2. Albert-László Barabási, *Linked: The New Science of Networks* (Cambridge, Mass.: Perseus Publishing, 2002), 41–42, quoting Mark S. Granovetter, "The Strength of Weak Ties," *American Journal of Sociology* 78, (1973), 1360–1380.

3. Ibid., 15.

4. Steven Johnson, *Emergence: The Connected Lives of Ants, Brains, Cities, and Software* (New York: Scribner, 2001), 13.

5. Patrick Henry, *The Ironic Christian's Companion: Finding the Marks of God's Grace in the World* (New York: Riverhead Books, 1999), 149.

6. Kennon L. Callahan, *Small, Strong Congregations* (San Francisco: Jossey-Bass, 2000), 133. [*Small, Strong Congregations*, Kennon L. Callahan, copyright 2000 by Kennon L. Callahan. Reprinted by permission of John Wiley and Sons, Inc.]

7. Brennan Manning, *The Signature of Jesus* (Sisters, Ore.: Multnomah Books, 1996), 135.

8. Howard Rheingold, *Smart Mobs: The Next Social Revolution* (Cambridge, Mass.: Perseus Publishing, 2002), 178, quoting William Morton Wheeler, *Emergent Evolution and the Development of Societies* (New York: W. W. Norton, 1928). [Reprinted by permission of Perseus Book Publishers, a member of Perseus Books, L.L.C.]

9. Rheingold, *Smart Mobs*, 176–177, quoting Kevin Kelly, *Out of Control* (Reading, Mass.: Addison-Wesley, 1994) http://www.kk.org/outofcontrol/index.html (6 March 2002).

10. Buchanan, *Nexus*, 14.

11. David Weinberger, *Small Pieces Loosely Joined: A Unified Theory of the Web* (Cambridge: Mass.: Perseus Publishing, 2002), 59.

12. Etienne Wenger, Richard McDermott, and William M. Snyder, *Cultivating Communities of Practice: A Guide to Managing Knowledge* (Boston: Harvard Business School Press, 2002), 169, quoting S. Denning, *The Springboard: How Storytelling Ignites Action in Knowledge-Era Organizations* (Boston: Butterworth-Heinemann, 2001); H. M. Trice and J. M. Beyer, *The Cultures of Work Organizations* (Englewood Cliffs, N.J.: Prentice Hall, 1993).

13. Weinberger, *Small Pieces Loosely Joined*, 65.

14. Rheingold, *Smart Mobs*, 166.

+ Chapter 5: Trading Spaces

1. Erving Goffman, "The Presentation of Self in Everyday Life: Selections," in *The Production of Reality: Essays and Readings on Social Interaction*, 3rd ed. by Jodi O'Brien and Peter Kollock (Thousand Oaks, Calif.: Pine Forge Press, 2001), 240.

2. Edward T. Hall, *The Hidden Dimension* (New York: Anchor Books/Doubleday, 1966, 1982), 115.

3. Brent Staples, "Black Men and Public Space," in O'Brien and Kollock, *The Production of Reality*, 244.

4. Pamela Paul, *The Starter Marriage and the Future of Matrimony* (New York: Random House, 2002), 103.

5.   Nancy Hanner, "Demystifying the Adoption Option," *Newsweek* (February 10, 2003), 15. [Nancy Hanner, "Demystifying the Adoption Option," From *Newsweek*, February 10, 2003. All rights reserved. Reprinted by permission.]

6.   Rachel Simmons, *Odd Girl Out: The Hidden Culture of Aggression in Girls* (New York: Harcourt, 2002), 3.

7.   Paul, *The Starter Marriage*, 139, quoting David Popenoe in Monica Davey, "Perspective: On the Record: David Popenoe, Co-Director of the National Marriage Project," *Chicago Tribune* (August 1, 1999), 3.

8.   To read more, visit www.searchtobelong.com. You can find the article "Sex and the Four Spaces" in the library section of the site.

9.   Ray Oldenburg, *The Great Good Place: Cafés, Coffee Shops, Bookstores, Bars, Hair Salons, and Other Hangouts at the Heart of a Community* (New York: Marlowe & Company, 1999), 248, quoting Margaret Mead, "The American Family" in Huston Smith, ed., *The Search for America* (Englewood Cliffs, N.J.: Prentice-Hall, 1959), 119.

10.   Paul, *The Starter Marriage*, 123.

11.   Simmons, *Odd Girl Out*, 43.

12.   Linda Van Leuven, "What Does the Service Include?" in O'Brien and Kollock, *The Production of Reality*, 254.

13.   Garrison Keillor, *Lake Wobegon Summer 1956* (New York: Viking, 2001), 86–87.

14.   Matthew 13:24–30.

15.   Matthew 13:47–52.

16.   See Matthew 25.

17.   Luke 15:28–32.

18.   Matthew 8:5–13.

19.   Matthew 26:36–39.

20.   You can see some of the photographs on my Web site: www.searchtobelong.com

21.   John 19:25–27.

22.   Anna Quindlen, "Begone, Buzz! Be Still, Soul." *Newsweek* (December 30, 2002/January 6, 2003), 116.

+ **Chapter 6: Searching for a Front Porch**

1.   *The Evolution of the American Front Porch: The Study of an American Cultural Object,* http://xroads.virginia.edu/%7ECLASS/am483_97/ projects/cook/cultur.htm, quoting Rochlin, "The Front Porch," in *Home, Sweet Home,* retrieved May 5, 2003. [Used by permission of Scott Cook]

2.   James McMurtry, "Levelland," *Where'd You Hide the Body?* Columbia, 1995, compact disc.

3.   Cook, "The Cultural Significance of the American Front Porch," *The Evolution of the American Front Porch.*

4.   Charles C. Bohl, *Place Making: Developing Town Centers, Main Streets, and Urban Villages* (Washington, DC: ULI—the Urban Land Institute, 2002), x.

5.   Larry R. Ford, *The Spaces between Buildings* (Baltimore: The Johns Hopkins University Press, 2000), 202, 203, 205. [Ford, Larry R. The Spaces between Buildings, pp. 202, 203, 204, 205. „ 2002 The John Hopkins University Press. Reprinted with permission of the John Hopkins University Press.]

6.   Bob Marley/Curtis Mayfield, "One Love/People Get Ready," *Exodus,* 1977, vinyl.

7.   Nora Ephron, transcribed from the commentary to *You've Got Mail,* 1998. Burbank, Calif.: Warner Bros. Digital video disc.

8.   Bohl, *Place Making,* 59–60.

9.   Ford, *The Spaces between Buildings,* 204.

10.   Beth L. Bailey, *From Front Porch to Back Seat: Courtship in Twentieth-Century America* (Baltimore: Johns Hopkins University Press, 1989), 4.

+ Chapter 7: What Now? Finding Harmony

1. www.searchtobelong.com

2. Kennon L. Callahan, *The Future That Has Come: New Possibilities for Reaching and Growing the Grass Roots* (San Francisco: Jossey-Bass, 2002), 139. [The Future That Has Come: New Possibilities for Reaching and Growing Grass Roots, Kennon L. Callahan, copyright 2002 by Kennon L. Callahan. Reprinted by permission of John Wiley and Sons, Inc.]

3. Neale Donald Walsch, *Friendship with God: an uncommon dialogue* (New York: G. P. Putnam's Sons, 1999), 20.

+ *Index*

Explore more paradigms for the church in the postmodern world